EMOTION IN MOTION

TALES OF A STEWARDESS
TOUCHED UPON IN FICTION, NON-FICTION AND POETRY

ALEXANDRA H. RODRIGUES

Copyright © 2016 Alexandra H. Rodrigues

All rights reserved.

ISBN:10: 0692708987
ISBN-13: 978-0692708989

DEDICATION

This book is dedicated to everybody who ever worked for
Pan American World Airways and enjoyed it.

Also to all passengers who ever flew with one of the
Pan Am Clippers and enjoyed it.

As well as to all my friends who for years urged me
to write and publish this book.

My sincere thanks to Gloria Savini-Kraemer.
She encouraged me to stick to the task
of writing this book. Her assistance in formatting,
publishing and editing was immense.

PREFACE

Since my first day as a flight attendant in 1958,
I had made notes. I knew that one day
I would write about my time in the air.
It took me more than 50 years to realize that plan.
This book hits on the pleasures and agonies of
25 years up in the air spent in the service of
a most outstanding company.

The Airline is "Gone But Never Forgotten."
May this book contribute to its memory.

CONTENTS

Autobiography	1
Teen Angst	5
How I Got the Job	9
All Clear	13
One Year with the IGS	14
My First Stewardess Pin	20
His Decision	21
Now and Then	28
Spray Away the Germs	33
How I Met My Husband	34
Mr. Right	48
Tiger, Tiger	49
Monkey	50
Another First	52
Age Limit	54
Rules Have Reason	56
Last Day of Vacation	65
3,000 Letters	66
Excerpts From a Diary	87
Risen	109
Certificates	130
Management	134
Fairbanks, Alaska	146
Paris Memoir	148
Thinking of Food	151
Turkey-Turkey	155
In-flight Entertainment	157
At the Airport	163
Romance Hasn't Died	165
Missed Opportunity	168
FaceBook	170
Tears	181
Let Me Off the Birds	183

Autobiography

Conceived by mistake to join a World in turmoil, I was born 1933 in Berlin, Germany, in the house my grandfather had built. My childhood was plastered with losses. We lost the house as a consequence of the ongoing inflation. My favorite aunt died at the early age of 32. My father left because political unrest spread its winds of disaster.

The house my Grandfather built.

My mother had a big family. At that time, her relatives were old and feeble. Consequently, the park I visited most often was the cemetery. Without question, it was and still today is a very pretty and peaceful place. I did a lot of planting and watering there to keep the graves looking nice. I still can picture myself lugging rusty water cans from two city blocks away to our family plot.

My most cherished memories from that time is dancing Ballet in The Berlin Opera as well as the recollections of waiting for my Mom in the backstage of the Burg Theatre in Vienna. While she was earning our daily living on stage, I was having fun trying on theatrical shoes and hats.

I remember Kindergarten in Vienna and rides on the Riesenrad, the famous Ferris wheel in Vienna's Prater amusement park. Later when I was evacuated during WWII to Austria for a little longer than a year, I attended the lyceum (high school) there.

An exciting youth followed. I was back in Berlin. It was the years after the War and all was allowed. We had been lucky to belong to the American sector. I was babysitting for an American family who had moved into the villa next to us during the occupation of the Four Powers. From the PX, the American shopping center, they bought me a cotton dress with red stripes and white stars. My flag dress, I called it. It was so American.

I finished my education and got my first job, selling purses and umbrellas in an upscale boutique on the Kurfürstendamm, the Champs-Élysées of Berlin. It did not last long – guess I was not nice enough to the boss. My good looks opened doors for me fast but also had a downside. When I applied for the position of fur model, I was given a fur bikini and asked to try it on while a creepy, elderly guy was devouring me with his eyes. I left immediately – escaped would be the better description.

Next I got a position at a jeweler. A fancy storefront with a workshop in the back. It was interesting, I learned about gems and carats, the art of designing jewelry and the value of mine finds. The fear of a senior female employee that I might outshine her, put me on the street again. I spent a year at a business school, and completed a certificate in English from Cambridge University. I landed a job as typist with a Swedish franchise of C.E. Johansson of Eskilstuna in Berlin. It was discovered that I have technical talent, and I was sent to Sweden to learn the repair of measurement instruments needed by big factories like Siemens and Agfa.

In 1958 I was hired by Pan American as a Flight Attendant for the Inter German Service. A year later Pan Am sponsored

Leaving for America

me to come to America and fly out of New York. A life among the rich and famous began. During that career, which lasted for 25 years, I came to see the entire world with the exception of Australia. I met my husband of 50 years on one of my first flights and we were married in 1960. He spoiled me and always catered to me; he called himself my butler, chauffeur, cook and lover.

In 1972 I gave birth to a son. I have had serious encounters with the medical society. I was said to be on the verge of death six times. Well that is another story. My pregnancy was first labeled menopause.

My Husband Ray

Baby Raymond

Only when I fainted after having arrived on a flight to Rome, did our company doctor tell me the happy news saying, "You are pregnant!" that I was pregnant. I stopped flying and went into Management. Later on I returned to Flight Status.

In 1985 I became President and coordinator of the Barry Farber Language Club on Long Island. After Pan Am had folded, I chose Real Estate as a new career. By now I have switched my main interest to writing, and I am happy to say this gives me great satisfaction and true fulfillment.

Please enjoy what I have selected to share with you. ✈

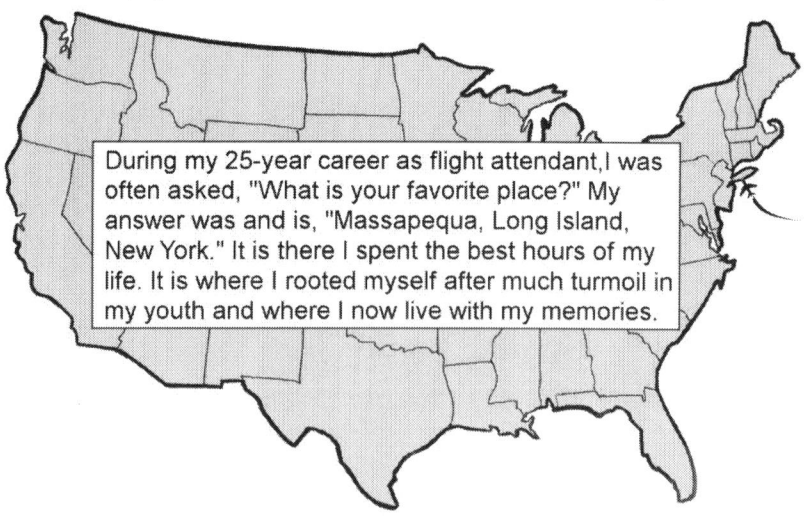

During my 25-year career as flight attendant, I was often asked, "What is your favorite place?" My answer was and is, "Massapequa, Long Island, New York." It is there I spent the best hours of my life. It is where I rooted myself after much turmoil in my youth and where I now live with my memories.

Teen Angst

My teenage years? They had followed a most confusing childhood. There were not too many illusions left. I was 13 years old when the War ended in 1946. Berlin had been freed. The terror of air attacks was over. No longer did I have to be afraid of being woken by shrill sirens. Those sirens had been the sign to grab some belongings, always readily packed in a little suitcase, and sneak into the bunker across from our house.

I had swallowed my first chewing gum, given to me by an American soldier when the Russians had finally left our area and we had become the American sector. That took place after I had witnessed rapes and destruction by the Russians. Still I had managed to save my family from starvation by venturing to a Russian Military Cantina and, dressed in a red jumpsuit, the Soviet color, begged for soup. The soup was rich and fatty.

I thumbed through some old letters recently, written in 1944 in Vienna to my grandmother in Berlin:

Dear Grandma,

How are you? Are you still sick? How is the food in Berlin? We just had a real air raid and went into the bunker. There were artillery shots, but not too bad. Hope I will find some nice shrapnel tomorrow for my collection.

Yes, I had been evacuated to Vienna in 1943. Presumably Vienna was safe! I was there in March 1944 when the first air raid destroyed most of the city – the City of Music of Strauss and his Waltzes, Franz Liszt and Mozart. At school in Vienna I received a "B" in music. Imagine that! In Berlin my report cards showed a "D" year after year. I deserved the "D." Truth is I cannot hold a note and never could.

This brings me to an event that occurred during my teen years: At the age of seven, I had joined a local dance school. Ms. Irene, the owner and instructor, taught us creative dancing. I loved it, and I was good at it. Eventually, I became the star of the group and the pet of Ms. Irene. At that time, I gave it no special thought that she made us run naked under the sprinkler in her garden.

When I was 11 years of age, two friends of mine, sisters, both in my dance class, decided to apply to the Berlin Opera. Their classes were free and students were also provided special allowances on food stamp cards.

"I am even better than they are," or so I thought, and went to apply. I was accepted. I hated it: Creative dance had been my strength – not Ballet! It was very strenuous, no room for imagination. I wanted to be a Ballerina! My grades in school plummeted. I began to dread the days I had Ballet class. Mrs. Merina obviously saw no merit in my dancing, and I did not like her a bit Then one day my pride got its ultimate shock. My mother awaited me with a letter from the Opera:

```
We regret to inform you that your daughter
Alexandra can no longer be supported by our
Ballet school as she has no ear for music.
Being musically talented is a requisite for
becoming a solo dancer.
```

I was devastated. I hated Mrs. Merina even more. It was my pride that was hurt most of all.

Well life has its ways. Ten years later, when I was already a Stewardess, I had Mrs. Merina as a passenger on the DC-4 from Berlin to Stuttgart. It was quite a bumpy flight. Mrs. Merina was afraid and got sick. With a typical Stewardess smile I handed her the airsick bag from the seat pocket. I mumbled, "I have to thank **you** for getting this fabulous job." And a little devil made me add, "Some people have no ear for music, and some people have no stomach for flying." She did not hear me – it did not matter. I had had my say.✈

How I Got the Job

This is the story about how I landed the job as Stewardess. At that time only about 10 out of 2,000 applicants were chosen. In my opinion, the gist of this story applies to all candidates for any job.

Some 20 heads turned and 40 eyes – green, blue, brown or hazel – evaluated me when I walked into the assigned suite of the Hilton Hotel in Berlin. I pulled up one of the folding chairs and nearly tore my left stocking in an effort to sit down gracefully. I was nervous, not at all sure of myself. When the clock of the nearby Kaiser Wilhelm Memorial Church, the well-known monument of Berlin, chimed three, not a chair was left empty. I counted 32 candidates, including myself. In the tense silence hanging in the room one could have heard a fingernail crack.

An exotic brunette and a pale blonde were skimming through *Vogue* and *Harpers* magazines, while the rest of us stared into the air. We were sizing each other up with measured side glances. All of us were curious about what was happening behind the closed door where the hiring committee of Pan American World Airways was holding court.

- ✈ Age 21 and over
- ✈ Weight depending on height (135 pounds for my height of 5.6)
- ✈ Height 5.4 to 5.8
- ✈ Must be bilingual or better
- ✈ Must have high school diploma or preferably college degree

Those were the basic requirements. I had seen the ad from Pan Am in the morning paper. On the spur of the moment I had called in sick to my oh-so-boring job as a secretary. I was going to give it another go. Being a Stewardess was a highly desirable job during those days and I had tried for the wings in the air with Lufthansa and TWA. Lufthansa turned me down because of my non-existent French and TWA because they could not sponsor me as they had no service out of Berlin.

A look into my hand mirror assured me that I was neatly groomed. The navy suit enhanced my figure. I had spent far over my budget for it. It resembled the style of the Pan American uniform, the reason why I had picked it.

One by one, the candidates were called. There seemed to be a pattern. Those who only spent a short time inside, came back out with an unhappy demeanor about them. A few who had spent longer inside looked rather pleased. My pondering about this fact was interrupted by one girl, who had been inside telling another candidate who probably was her girlfriend, "They want to know what the capital of Alaska is. Beats me. So I guess it is over for me."

My palms got sweaty. Damn it. A vision of Dr. Luedke, my high school geography teacher, flashed thru my mind: "Girls pay attention." I hadn't. Now I was drawing a blank. I had to do something. Who would know? My mother! I rushed to the phone booth which was close by. While I was still dialing I heard my name being paged. The receiver nearly dropped to the floor, I had to untangle myself from the cord and slammed the handset back into the cradle.

Without haste I made my way to the interview. A lost cause for sure, so the quicker I got it over with the better. Numb, I found myself facing a panel of three important looking men and an elegant older lady – the Chief Stewardess as I would later find out.

"Is something wrong?" the gray-haired man with horn-rimmed glasses inquired.

I blurted out, "I know you are asking what the capital of Alaska is. Well, I do not know, but I tried to find out. You paged me before I could get the answer from my mother."

To my surprise everybody laughed. Totally deflated, I now thought I had made a fool of myself on top of everything. The lady offered me a seat. Questions which I remembered from the previous interviews at other airlines were put to me:

"Do you like flying?"
"Do you like people?"
"Are you willing to relocate should it become necessary?"

I answered honestly and without embellishment. Then it was over. They all stood up simultaneously. With a jovial smile, the man who had originally greeted me came over and shook my hand.

"You will get a letter from us in about a week," he said.

I knew or thought I knew what he referred to. I had received two letters before. Both starting with "Sorry, we regret…"

I have no way to describe the surprise I felt when he added, "You will be accepted. Welcome to Pan Am."

Was I dreaming? For sure – I was stunned. Today after many years of flying I understand that they had hired me because I came across unpresumptuous, and when in a bind I would know how to take initiative to resolve a crisis.

My advice: Keep cool, be honest and don't throw in the hat unless you are told "No."

There is always a chance for a "**Yes**." ✈

All Clear

The planes came so close
Up in the sky at twenty thousand feet
It seemed that hands we could hold
If so we chose
At impact our screams would meet.

It was over in less than a second
Two pilots, two planes
A correct decision had beckoned
Free cruising, unblemished sight
Assured that all was again well and right.

One Year in the Inter-German Service

My first year flying with the Inter-German Service was 1958-1959. I have little documentation about places I travelled then because I would return to home base every night. My home base was Berlin, so I lived at my family house with little difference to my daily routine.

In 1954, Pan American, Air France and British Airways had opened air traffic out of Berlin into West Germany. This was to facilitate connections between the divided country. The Russians could not fly into West Germany. They maintained their own airport in East Berlin. The Russian Zone presented complications for ground traffic.

My little red Goggomobile

My residence was in the American Sector of Berlin. With my little red Goggomobile (not much bigger than a sewing machine with a hood over it), I proudly drove to report for my flights at Tempelhof Airport. It was years earlier that my grandmother had taken me to just that same spot, the airfield where I admired the first commercial airplane. War planes up in the air I had seen many, many more than I wish to remember. This was different: elegant little DC-4s, Connies and American military planes. It was a one-hour ride by public transportation from Zehlendorf, the suburb where I live, to this airfield. Quite a distance for Berlin. This was long before I learned of the long stretches between points A and B, which I later came to master in New York.

All my flights out of Berlin were turn-arounds. The longest flight was about one hour and 20 minutes from Berlin to Stuttgart. The shortest flight was Berlin to Hanover, a 35-minute flight.

The cities we flew to:

>BLN Berlin
>FRA Frankfurt
>STU Stuttgart
>HAN Hanover
>MUC Munich
>DUS Düsseldorf
>HAM Hamburg
>COL Cologne

The airplane on all trips was a DC-4 with capacity for 62 passengers. No life vests. No oxygen masks. We served sandwiches on all of those flights and there was always enough provision to take some home. It was still the time of the airbags: Those sickening brown sturdy paper bags. Their smell when full still revolts me when I think of it today.

How lax the rules about visiting the cockpit were at that time. Many times the cockpit doors remained opened in flight. It was not unusual that I was allowed to sit in the First Officer's seat and was even permitted to a handle the controls for a few seconds.

Dressed for success in the IGS

We were assigned 70 flight hours on a monthly basis which gave us plenty of free time at home. The flights had two pilots, a Captain and First Officer.

Many of them had flown the Air Corridor dropping food into Berlin. We called the planes the Rosinen (raisin) Bombers. The function called luftbrücke. The provisions they brought into Berlin were like sweet nourishing raisins. Most of our pilots had earned their certification with the American Air Force during WW II.

The Inter-German Service flights were often very turbulent. Due to regulations, the pilots were required to fly within a very narrow corridor. In bad weather, thunder or snowstorms, they were still required to stay in the corridor; no diversion was allowed. Often we had Russian military jets tracking us to check the compliance with these regulations.

One interesting route took us over Wittenberg – a city on the River Elbe southwest of Berlin. In good weather we could see the cathedral where the religious reformer Martin Luther is said to have nailed his theses against the process of selling indulgences in October 1531. When we told the passengers about it, they all went to one side of the airplane to see the sight and the airplane tilted that way.

Coming back to Berlin from all points west, we had to approach the landing runway by flying over a cemetery. At that point the plane was many times so low that we could see the graves and nearly read the inscriptions on the memorial stones. At the same time the noise of the landing gear extending would signal the end of the flight and extinguish any morbid thoughts.

There were always two Flight Attendants on board. No male cabin attendants or black Stewardesses at that time. We were like a family, and most of us came to know each other after a short while. I flew the IGS for exactly one year. It was a good introduction to what would become a more intensified lifestyle for many years. I was admired by most of my friends. Of course, there were also those, being jealous, called a flying waitress.

There were no trips to interesting cities in the IGS, no layovers in foreign countries. So when the opportunity offered itself to transfer to an International base of the airline, it was a fabulous opportunity. I had to go through a harrowing procedure to pass the qualifications to be considered.

Perfect knowledge of the English language was required. A rather snippy answer of mine given to the interviewing panel got me the job despite not being fluent in English. To the remark of the hiring committee that my English fluency left something to be desired, my answer was "flying your Inter-German Service where everybody speaks German does not really lend itself to polish one's language skills. I can assure you that once I am in the United States and exposed to the English language on a daily basis, I will become fluent in no time."

That was a great chance I had taken. Luckily it worked. ✈

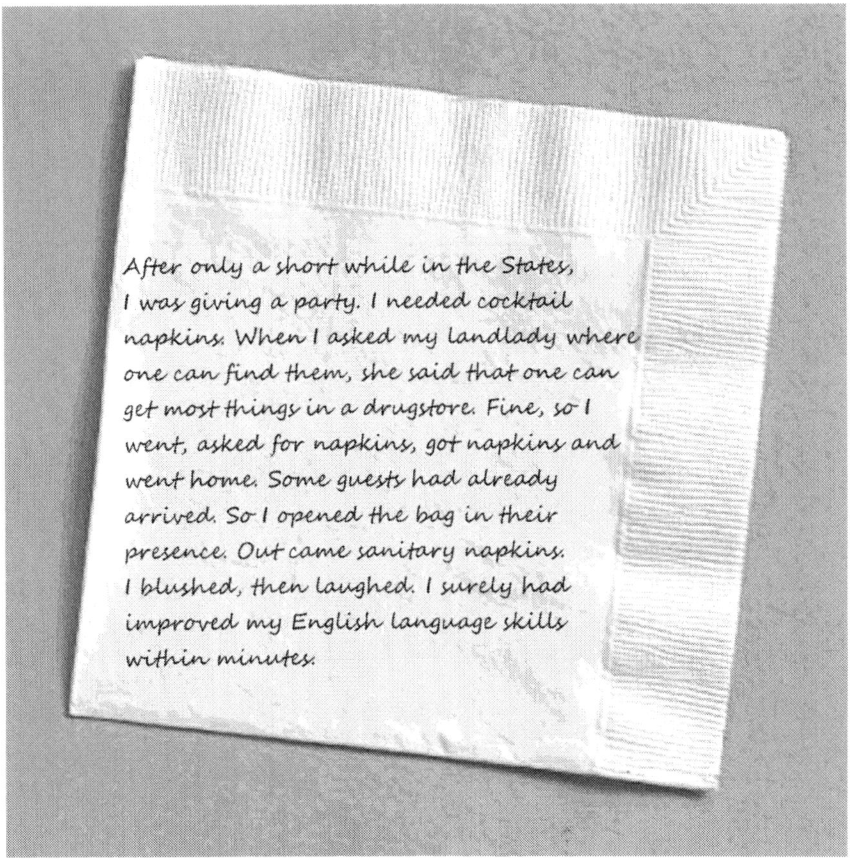

After only a short while in the States, I was giving a party. I needed cocktail napkins. When I asked my landlady where one can find them, she said that one can get most things in a drugstore. Fine, so I went, asked for napkins, got napkins and went home. Some guests had already arrived. So I opened the bag in their presence. Out came sanitary napkins. I blushed, then laughed. I surely had improved my English language skills within minutes.

My First Stewardess Pin

I began my career as Stewardess declaring, "I'll do it for a year." Next I decided my year in the Inter-German Service did not count. The one year I had planned on was meant for international service out of New York or any other base in the United States. That one year turned into 25 years. It was only terminated because Pan Am went Chapter 11. A sad ending for a once so proud airline now remembered by many as *Gone but never forgotten*.

In 1958, it was quite difficult to land a job as a stewardess. Only 2 percent of applicants were hired out of 2,000 young aspiring ladies.

As they attached the stewardess pin to my pale blue, snugly fitting uniform (we had to wear girdles or be removed from flight), I felt proud as a peacock and clacked away in my high-heeled black pumps (flats were only allowed if one had been assigned to the airplane galley). I would parade among as many people as I could find for them to see me as full-fledged Flight Attendant. I had gotten my wings and now I would fly, really truly fly and so I did.

Even now as an old lady, I still wear my pin at times. I remain proud to have been a Flight Attendant and proud of the airline that had chosen me to serve them. ✈

His Decision

This story is fiction. It borders greatly on possibility in the airlines and could easily have been taken from real life.

The altimeter on the instrument panel of the Boeing 707 showed 6,000 feet.

They had left their cruising altitude of 35,000 feet a few moments ago, and Roy maneuvered the plane down skillfully to save fuel. According to the navigation chart they were now 63 miles from Detroit Metro Airport. Suburban homes and cars, bumper to bumper on the highway, could already be clearly distinguished. Trying to sound lighthearted, as he watched the needle of the fuel gauge coming uncomfortably close to zero, Jim, the co-pilot, said, "I wish we were on the ground."

Today, Roy McNeil did not experience the usual thrill from being the commander of a commercial airliner. Tall and broad shouldered, his flaxen hair brushed back from a tanned baronial face, he presented the perfect image of a handsome Captain. Only 42, he had made it to Captain with an airline where many men were flying as First Officers till close to retirement.

While his eyes searched routinely along the milky blue sky for nearby traffic, his conscience nagged him because of the decision he had made a little while ago. He had acted against better judgment. For the first time he had allowed private interests to interfere with duty. Roy's thoughts centered on Elena: Elena Lancer, a green-eyed fashion model. Because of his courtship with her, he was now forcing his luck.

When they had left Shannon, Ireland, some seven hours ago, the flight plan had called for a fuel stop in Montreal, Canada. Then during the crossing, the winds had picked up and although the fuel calculation had still indicated that a refueling stop was advisable, Elena's spell over him had made him decide against it.

Flying straight into Detroit, he could catch an American Airline flight and make it to New York today. He could virtually feel her arms around him. How he wanted to be with her. They would drown in dreams about Mandalay, fantasize about the future. Their longing for each other would merge them in embraces till the early morning hours. Today was Elena's birthday. Her request that he be with her seemed childish, but it was flattering. Only if they made Detroit non-stop and he could catch the American Airline flight, would it work out.

When he had announced over the intercom to the 158 passengers on board that they would fly directly into Detroit, there had been cheers. How could they know that he gambled with their safety?

A glance at his watch, a Skymaster always set by Greenwich Time, showed 2:30 Detroit time. He should be on the ground at 3:50 the latest. He could be in New York by 5 pm – plenty of time to celebrate. With a fuel stop, he would miss the connection to New York and have to wait till the following day. He visualized Elena in his arms exactly the way they had planned it, or rather the way Elena had planned it. Was it really only two months ago that he had met her? His friend's remark, "There is your match," had been an understatement. His friends always envied his success with women and his ability to steer clear of marriage. No girl had ever held his interest for long. Elena was different. First he

A Pan American 707

had been intrigued by her aloof attitude only to become amazed at the treasure of loving stimulation she displayed after he had managed to arouse her interest. Holding her slim body in his arms he experienced the sensation of being drugged. This effect didn't wear off when they were apart.

"This is Detroit Center, Flight 469 descend and maintain 5,000 feet," the message from the tower cut into his daydreaming and he heard Jim acknowledge immediately, "Roger, Flight 469. We'll descend and maintain 5,000 feet, awaiting further clearance." Jim was one of the men who had been recently hired after completing a tour with the Air Force in Vietnam. He was a good flyer, who also knew to respect his place and the decisions of the man on his left.

Roy massaged an aching muscle in his right shoulder just below the neck, a result of his own days in the field during WW II. He had been drafted. It had not been his choice.

Fifteen minutes till touchdown. There was sufficient fuel to make the landing, and the landing was his. With his landings there was never a worry about a go-around or aborted landing. Yet it was standard procedure to count on the unforeseen. A landing gear could get stuck or another plane could block the approach pattern.

They were flying through an area of crosswinds, losing valuable seconds. The plane quivered, bouncing spasmodically.

"There is the airport on the right. Shall we ask for a visual approach?" Jim asked. That remark showed that he was well aware of the fuel shortage. Roy answered without enthusiasm, "If there is no traffic we might as well."

Sweat pearls formed on Roy's forehead. No one to blame for this quandary except Elena and her damn appeal, he thought. An instrument landing with the fuel dangerously low against a visual approach in haze and smog wasn't much of a choice. The last rays of the sun flooded the cockpit with pale orange.

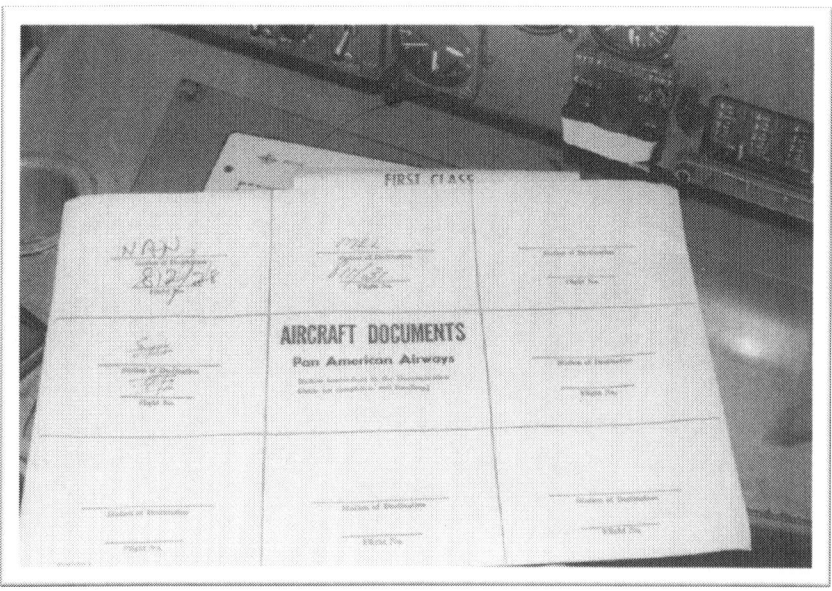

"Forget about Elena. Pay attention," Roy cautioned himself and locked his seat into position for landing.

"Cleared visual. No traffic ahead," Jim repeated a ground message and added, "No go-around now, boss."

"That's for sure," Roy grimly gave credit to his co-pilot's stable nerves

The jet touched down smoothly. The low-pressure lights on the engineer panel flashed when Roy pushed the engines into reverse. They were sucking the last margin of fuel. Through the walls of the locked cockpit door came the sound of clapping from the passenger cabin. Roy let go of the wheel and exhaled deeply. His decision had passed without consequence, but that he had taken this risk bothered him.

It was shortly past 4 pm when he checked his baggage through customs. There was plenty of time left to make the plane to New York.

"I'll call Elena now, give her a little hello – a big hello later," he thought and went into the telephone booth. Then he heard her voice, so melodious and also a trifle funny with the French accent she was trying to cultivate ever since her recent visit to Paris. He thought he could smell her tantalizing perfume while she greeted him.

"Oh, hello, mon ami. You made it. I knew you would come."

She had known, hadn't she? His irritation grew. It was her fault that he'd acted irresponsibly, that he'd lost track of what was right. She was corroding him. His mouth tightened, he frowned, and again he made a decision. With closed eyes he shouted into the phone.

"Elena, I am NOT coming to see you."

Quickly before she could answer, he hung up and stepped outside into the crowd of pushing and rushing travelers.

"There! I've shown her," He muttered silently. "Now she can no longer influence me."

At customs he declared the perfume he had bought for Elena. Suddenly he felt very tired. Would Elena cry now? Good! No, not good! Was it really she who had made him act out of line? Or was it his desire for her? Actually she was not to blame for his decision. She did not even know what had happened.

In vain he tried to erase her nearly perfect figure and her always so tender smile from his mind when somebody tapped him on the shoulder. He turned around. It was Jim, who said, "Guess what. I just called New York. Congratulate me! My wife gave birth to a baby boy: 6 pounds, 4 ounces. We'll call him Max. Great you got us home today."

Hearing that, Roy's train of thought changed. He had played with other people's lives. That newborn child could have lost his father before ever meeting him.

"Congratulations! You'll make a great father." He had played God. It was not Elena's fault at all, and now he was nearly making another wrong decision. Nobody was to blame but himself. He would have to cope with his guilt alone. He had learned his lesson, and to himself he confessed his mistake.

Still pensive, he remembered a flower shop on the second floor of the terminal. He ran up the steps and called out to the sales girl, "Hurry, my plane is leaving in a few minutes. Give me the 12 longest and reddest roses you can find. I have to make up to my girlfriend."

He was not sure yet if he would share the experience with Elena. Maybe one day. He did not want her to be afraid every time he was going on a flight.

He looked skyward and sent a silent prayer of thanks to the power that had helped to avoid a catastrophe. ✈

Now and Then

Now is today as I write this. But tomorrow, now is already then.

I saw my first airplanes during World War II: They were American C-47s and B-24s that bombed Berlin, and German FW 191s that patrolled the area. Today the most advanced fighter plane in production is the F-22.

After the War, I saw a commercial plane when my grandmother took me to Tempelhof, the now dormant airport in Berlin. It was a Douglas DC-3, appearing gigantic to me when I saw it lift up into the air with its two propellers noisily accelerating and heading out of the city, over the cemeteries which nearly bordered the runways. As stewardess, many years later, flying the Inter-German Service during the Berlin Airlift, I clearly remember being able to see all those graves on approach to the runway.

Like many other airports in the world, the runways originally built at Tempelhof were too short for the powerful machines of the Jet Age. Many airports had to be closed, and new larger ones were built away from the cities.

Military two-seater biplanes already existed during the First World War. Commercial travel was inaugurated in the United States about 1925 with KLM and Lufthansa existing as airlines in embryonic form.

Juan Trippe (who later became the first president of Pan American World Airways) opened the first U.S. airline called Long Island Airways. It collapsed. Mail routes flown by airplanes sprung up everywhere and pilots flew in open planes at low altitudes. Juan Trippe took a single-engine seaplane, carrying mail 90 miles from Key West to Havana, and expanded the operation into the vast world-wide airline Pan American.

In 1935, the first Flying Boat left San Francisco to cross the Pacific Ocean. It would take pages to describe the models of planes that followed during the next years: DC-3, DC-4, DC-6 and DC-7 as well as the Douglas 8, the Connie, the Boeing 377, which we as flight crew called the Pregnant Oyster. Finally, Mr. Trippe brought the airline into the Jet Age in the 1950s. My first flight to Johannesburg, South Africa, took 32 hours one way on a DC-6. Nowadays a jet can take that distance in 12 hours.

My neighbor, a retired Federal Aviation Administration inspector in his 80s, recalls, "My father takes me to an airfield to see a World War I flyer perform at the farmer's cornfield. The pilot asks the people if they would like to go for a ride, for just a small cost. The plane is a front and back two-seater. I go. People are watching as he lashes me into the front seat and away we go. I am in awe. Mouth wide open, about to throw up, as the air rushes in. He sees it and tells me to shut my mouth. Some stunt flying and return to the corn strip. I never lost my passion for flying after that."

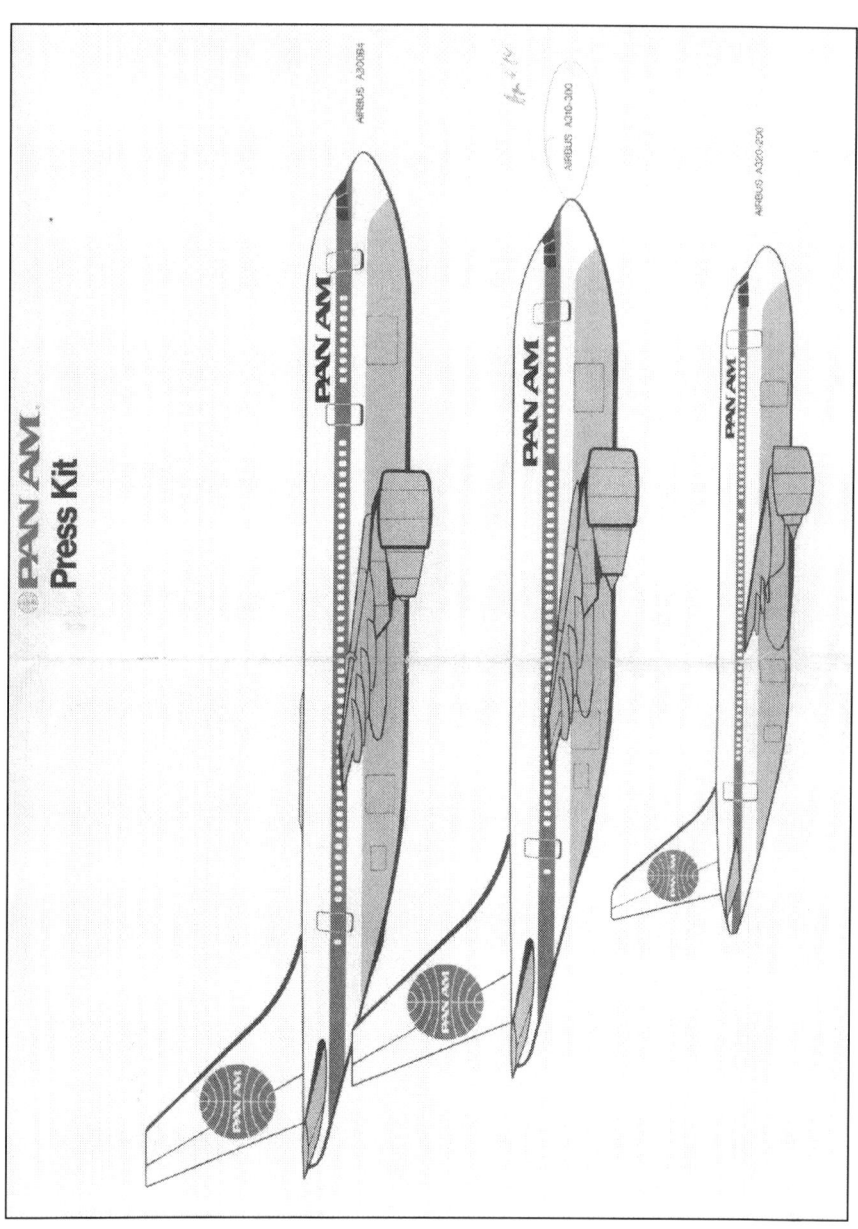

Another interesting comment I got from an older lady: "The first time I saw an airplane was when I was a little girl at a Beach Club in New Rochelle. There was a man with a seaplane (Piper Cub) who gave rides for $5. My mother let me go up for a ride and I was thrilled."

Plane sizes and functions have changed dramatically during the past decades. So have the rules. For many years, we were allowed to invite VIPs into the cockpit. Many times the doors to the cockpit were left open letting First Class passengers see the pilots. Next the doors had to be kept closed. Finally came the time when we were given a cockpit key, and only the Chief Flight Attendants were allowed to enter during the flight. Did things get better? You decide.

Nowadays the average number of people airborne over the U.S. in any given hour is 61,000. Today, the most recent commercial airliners are the Boeing 787, and the Airbus 350 and 380. The A380 is the latest and the greatest for the Airbus fleet. In the military world, the Lockheed

Martin/Boeing F-22 Raptor and the Lockheed Martin F-35 are the most modern.

The Boeing 787 Dreamliner had its first scheduled flight in October 2011 flying from Tokyo to Hong Kong in 4.5 hours. It can accommodate 290 passengers. The program had been launched in April 2004 with a record order from All Nippon Airways. By 2011, six continents placed orders, totaling 821 airplanes at about $145 billion making it the most successful twin-aisle launch of a new commercial airplane in Boeing history.

Boeing 797 can seat 1,000!?

What does the future of flying hold? While the Boeing 797 is just an internet hoax, does it foreshadow where aviation is headed? The hoax boasts 1,000-passenger capacity in a blended body. ✈

Spraying the Germs Away

Nowadays the Zika Virus is a true threat to unborn babies. Zika is unresponsive to antibiotics and causes deformation of the skull in unborn babies when a woman is exposed to it during pregnancy. Participants and spectators at Brazil's 2016 Olympics feared spreading the virus to their homelands

This makes me wonder why we stopped spraying with the aerosol bombs before landing. Each flight from a foreign country entering the US had to be sprayed. We made an announcement about 15 minutes prior landing:

"Ladies and gentlemen, the US Health regulations require that the aircraft cabin be sprayed before arrival. The spray has an odd smell but is harmless to humans. The smell will dissipate within a few minutes."

We would then take the small spray bottle and walk through the cabin, spraying the aerosol till the bottle was empty. At the port of entry, officials from the Health Department would enter the aircraft through a narrowly opened cabin door. We would hand the officials the spray container. They checked that it was empty and only then were we allowed to open all the doors. Why this procedure was terminated a long time ago I do not know. It had made sense to me. ✈

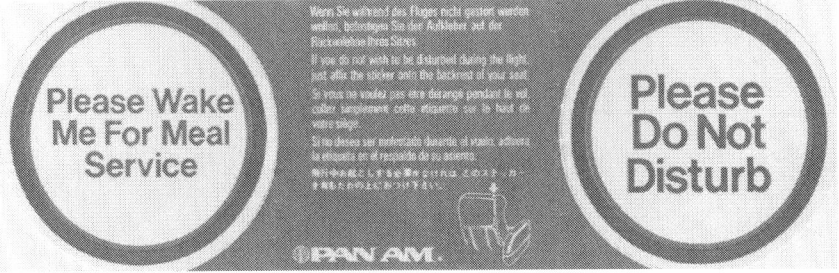

How I Met My Husband

His Story

When asked how we met, my husband was always the one who answered:

"She was a cute kid with pigtails asking for chewing gum. I was a paratrooper, and right after D-Day I came to Berlin, where Alexandra lived with her mother. I got friendly with them, and before I was to leave to go back to the States, I promised I would stay in touch and sponsor Alexandra when she turned 18 years. That time, in Berlin, she just had celebrated her 12th birthday. Well, she was already in her twenties when we got all the papers together, but I made it happen. I got her a job and a place to stay and assisted her to get acquainted with America."

There had been no thought in my mind about us getting married. But we saw each other quite a few times, began to truly like each other and here we are, a happily married couple.

We stayed married for 50 years until my husband was called into heaven. However, the story told by him, is not at all true. He was in Berlin. I was in Berlin. But we had not met at that time.

The Prediction

An occurrence that neither my husband nor I ever forgot made me believe in the psychic powers of some people for sure.

At the time when I worked my first flights out of JFK, Mary Wilson was a purser, as was my husband. I believe the flight in question was to Lisbon, Portugal. She and my husband had flown together previously. Both of them were language-qualified in Portuguese. Ray did not know me at all and neither did Mary. However, her words to Ray were, "There is a stewardess working Economy Class. She is the girl you are going to marry."

And so it came to be. Mary died at a relatively young age but we never forgot her prediction, which at the time she made it, was so unlikely to become fact.

Make Believe Honeymoon

One day, Ray and I were assigned to pick up a charter flight from Buffalo Niagara International Airport and to work it to Rome.

We were to deadhead via American Airlines. Niagara Falls is a famous honeymoon spot. The plane was full, so Ray and I did not get seats together. We were travelling in civilian clothes and the American Airline crew had no way of knowing that we were playing a game to get seats together.

"Stewardess we are on our honeymoon. Could you find us seats together?" I pleaded, and it worked. Once sitting next to each other, we had to hold hands and snuggle up. It felt good and so it all began.

His Girlfriend

I had taken a ride to The Bronx where Ray lived with his mother. We had been assigned to fly the same pattern of flights for the entire month. By that time, I had an eye on Ray. He seemed interested in me, too. He acted as if he loved me but never said it.

So I was going to surprise him. I was also curious how he lived and exactly where. When I drove up to his address, Paulding Avenue, The Bronx, I parked in front of the two-family attached house.

When I rang the bell, an elderly woman in a house coat, with white hair greeted me in broken English.

"He is not here. Went to see his girlfriend. That whore in Jersey."

I was shell-shocked: His girlfriend?

A friendly conversation began and I vaguely remember that she asked me lots of questions.

"Wait a moment," she suddenly said and left the nicely furnished living room, where we had been sitting.

When she returned, she took my left hand and pressed a ring into my palm with the comment, "I want my son to marry you."

The ring was her engagement ring. White gold with tiny diamonds!!!

The Surprise Engagement

The year was 1960. There was going to be a party! A party in the basement of the house on North Cottage Street in Valley Stream. There we, later called The Three Queens by my husband, rented the upstairs of an extended Cape Cod home. Ingrid Gabrielli, Dorothea Rilk and me. All three of us were Pan Am stewardesses.

Ingrid did the decorations. Dorothea arranged for a deejay. I briefed the invited guests on the special plan for this party. Only one person, the groom-to-be Ray, had no idea what was the reason for the celebration: His and my engagement party!

On the way to the party, I had asked him to pick up several Pan Am people.

It could not have worked out better. As soon as all the guests had arrived, I gave the pre-arranged sign and people began to congratulate Ray. "Congratulate me for what?" he asked. It took a few "All the best" wishes till it dawned on Ray what a joke had been played on him. Luckily, Ray's kindness and our good peach punch left no room for any annoyance on his side. It turned out to be a great party.

Of course, I never got a proposal from my future husband! I had taken care of that by giving this party. And an engagement ring, the one his mother had given me, I had already, too. A fact that seemed to astonish Ray even more than the party.

The Three Queens

Dorothea Bruneaux nee Rilk was the prettiest among us, yet she forced her well-proportioned figure into corsets and other shapewear. She was critical of us, her roommates, but mostly of herself. She was the first of us to get married. She married a Parisian. He was short and wiry, and she called him her Hutzelmännchen. She quit flying shortly after her marriage, and they had a child Bettina. A divorce and many unfortunate occurrences foiled her life. She died young.

Ingrid Lubienecki nee Gabrielli, still my best friend, is Austrian. She is called by many the "Smiling Austrian." The person who does not like Ingrid is yet to be born. She loved flying and she shied no work. Mostly she worked the galley. Close to food and Champagne, she was in her element. This caused her frequent weight checks. She was the last to marry. It was not due to a lack of admirers. Her husband, also still living, is a Polish Count. Born in Innsbruck, Ingrid loves the mountains. She kept flying till the end of Pan

The Three Queens: Dorothea, Alexandra and Ingrid

American, and shuttled among her three houses: One in Innsbruck, one in Babylon, NY, and the main residence with her husband in Syracuse, NY. Due to her extremely pleasant personality and her fluency in three languages, she was often called upon to serve on special press charters.
Ingrid had been chosen as crew member on a charter that accompanied Air Force One with President Eisenhower. At several airports, the Pan Am Press Charter was scheduled to

land shortly before Air Force One. The Pan Am crew had to form a guard of honor around the film crews present to take pictures of the President's arrival. In Teheran the streets and airport area were covered with Persian carpets for the occasion. Many onlookers crowded the streets for the celebration.

Ingrid went on the Sukarno Charter, a Pan Am 707 jet, for a United Nations meeting. Sukarno had chartered it crew inclusive for $20 million in 1960. Sukarno was the first President of Java. He was born on June 6, 1901 and died in 1970. He had held the position of president for 21 years.

On the Sukarno Charter the stewardesses each received a roll of silk during their stop in Tokyo. He gave it to Ingrid saying she should use it to have a wedding dress made from it. She did that. As a matter of fact she took the silk with her, eight years later, on a Flight to Hong Kong. There the Melwani tailor that did all the dresses and suits for the crew members of Pan Am created a simple, classically beautiful dress for her.

One of the Sukarno charters on which Ingrid was serving, took them on a roundtrip from Jakarta to Jakarta with stops in like Karachi, San Francisco, Acapulco, Tokyo, Cuba, the Philippines and others. A nearly 6-week trip.

Ingrid and each of the other cabin crew were also given a large silver bowl and other presents during and at the end of this charter. As Flight Attendants we were strictly forbidden to accept gratuities, but since it was not a commercial flight the rules did not really apply.

On commercial flights, the public was mostly aware of the regulations and very seldom would a passenger try to stick some money into our aprons at the end of a dinner service. When it happened it felt quite awkward having to return it, but we did. Twice I remember having gotten presents which we kept because they were sent to our home address. My husband got a case of wine from Mr. Perillo, the founder of the Perillo charters and I received a three-string pearl bracelet from a partner of the Mikimoto pearls empire.

Alexandra and Dorothea with 1951 Chevy.

Our transportation from Valley Stream to Idlewild, the then name of John F. Kennedy Airport, was a 1951 Chevy. Its air conditioning was provided by rusty holes in the floor. Its audio was a handheld transistor radio.

Right and left signals were given by waving our arms outside of the manually operated windows.

One day Ingrid got stuck with this beauty in the Midtown Tunnel. It won her a spot on the local news. Another time she was stopped for speeding. She was on the way to the house my husband and I owned in the Bronx. She was wearing only a teeny-weeny bikini and had her water skis tied on top of the roof. Again her charm won, and she was not issued a ticket. She had managed to stop traffic in the Midtown Tunnel.

Even before Ingrid joined Pan American, she had some experiences that would leave some young girls in awe. She curtsied for the Queen of England and was courted by an Italian attaché.

Ingrid also flew the Shah of Persia from Tehran to Paris. The Shah was married to Farah Diva who was with him on that trip and Ingrid served them in First Class. Later, negotiations about the Shah pulling Pan American out of debt did not materialize.

In addition, during her flight career Ingrid met Ingrid Bergman (Ingrid also mentions her as her namesake), and Grace Kelly who was married to Prince Rainier III of Monaco.

My personal meetings with well-known people include:

- **Maria Callas.** She could not be bothered with holding on to 50 red roses given to her by shipping magnate Aristotle Onassis upon departure from Rome.
- **Walt Disney.** I met him as a good looking, distinguished passenger on one of my Inter German flights. He gave me an autograph on the inside of my first Pan American shoulder bag. Unfortunately, that bag got lost. I wish I still had it.
- **Stephen King.** We had time to talk for a while. When I mentioned my interest in writing, he predicted that I would do well. How he could come to this conclusion during our short conversation, I do not know. I'm happy to say, "Thank you Mr. King. Your words have been heard by the power of destiny."
- **Charles Kálmán.** (son of Emmerich Kálmán best known for the opera *Maritza*). The composer and I became good friends.
- **The Supremes.** They impressed me most by their identical leather coats in three different colors. I had the pleasure of hanging up those coats in our Pan American coat room.
Albert Schweitzer. Doctor, theologist and missionary.
- **Wilhelm Furtwängler.** German conductor and composer considered to be one of the greatest symphonic and operatic conductors of the 20th century.
- **Jackie Kennedy.** We met during a transit in Ireland.

Charles Kálmán

✈ **Ted Kennedy**. On the flight I had him, he chose to fly Economy Class. He provided me with an autograph on a A mistake I am realizing only just now. After all it is not fair to be handed a First Class menu when you have to eat an Economy meal.

Ted Kennedy's signature at center bottom.

✈ On our crew bus I often met actress **Maureen O'Hara** on her way to meet Charles Bennett, a very attractive Pan American Captain.
✈ During my time in Germany I took a ride on the backseat of a motorcycle owned by actor **Kurt Maisel**.
✈ When in Limerick, Ireland, I enjoyed lunch with **Mirette Hanley-Corboy**, who later became well-known for her contributions to construction and education in Ireland.

✈ **The Beatles.** Pan Am brought them to New York for their first performance in the States when Ed Sullivan introduced them to America.

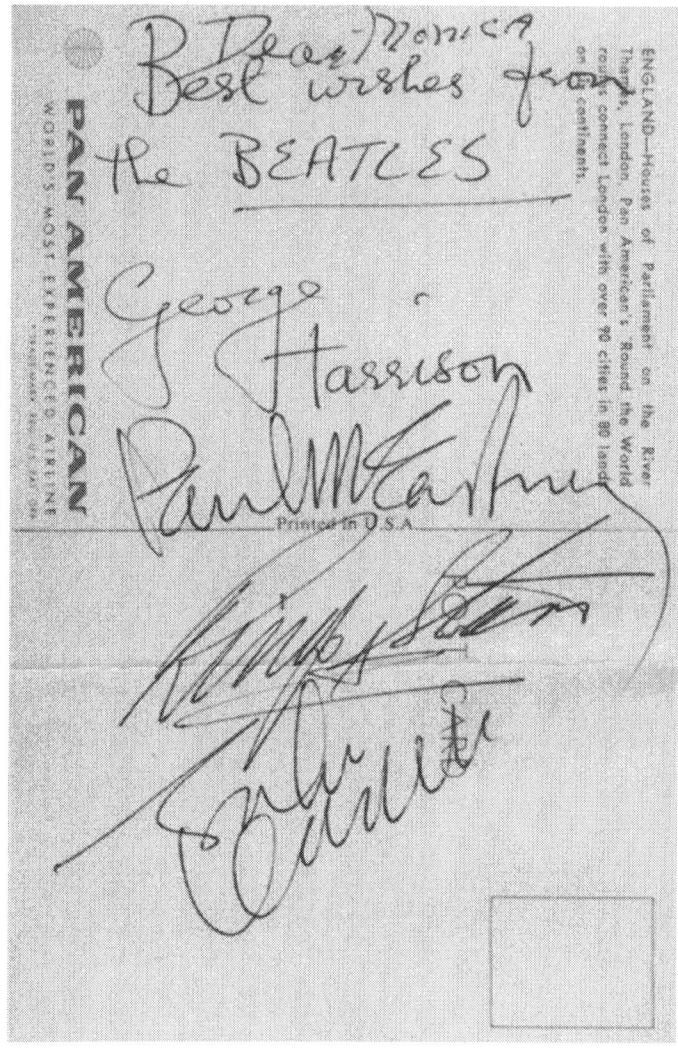

✈ During my time in management, I got to know talk show host **Barry M. Farber**. He is an American conservative radio talk show host, author and language learning enthusiast. He ran for Conservative Party nominee for Mayor of New York City in 1977, preceded by Maria Biaggio and succeeded by John Esposito as Conservative Party nominee for the position. After the fall of Pan Am, I was selected by Barry Farber to run his language clubs on Long Island. The Language Club was a stimulating, well-educated, interesting, fun group of people from all walks of life. People who enjoy speaking foreign languages. It was open to any body regardless of fluency in language and quite an opportunity to learn while making new friends.✈

PO BOX 121 TIMES SQUARE STATION NEW YORK, N.Y. 10108 (212) 787-2110

Mister Right

Prince Charming I at one time did meet
With his fabulous figure in his sport cabriolet
He all my other admirers beat.

You guessed it: he was good for a fling
But from the start I knew it could not last forever
Thus just a little while of lust and thrills I did sing.

So I rode on his horse
And of course of real love he never spoke
Which I had known and felt no remorse.

I picked myself a solid man
Who for none of the playboys I would change.
He became my husband, my lover and my greatest fan.

Tiger, Tiger

The tiger was bothered by all the attention
Of kids, hoodlums and old folks on pension.
In front of the cage they were standing in awe
Watching the raw meat he held in his paw.
Tiger swore that he would stir up plenty of sand
When to their own food they did attend.

Mostly he minded a fresh young girl
She enacted loud barfing when his meat he would twirl.
Tiger decided to first take a piss
That girl with the leather jacket he could hardly miss.
So his hind leg he lifted
And watched how to its aim the urine drifted.

The girl screamed and everyone ran away.
The tiger now could have it all his way.
At the cleaners the girl was nastily laughed at
Asked if next time she'd claim a white whale had spat.

With anger and embarrassment, she turned blue
She would never again go and visit the zoo.
For which the tiger will be grateful too.

Monkey – Monkey

Born in a cage
Puck had no wish a challenge to wage.
Given the daily necessities
He had no desires, he did not search release.

Free monkeys came to visit from the outside
They tried to convince Puck to join their fight
Stressing that freedom is everybody's right
"I see it is hard for you to survive," said Puck
"Why should I give up my easy life and change my luck?

"Do you have no far-reaching goal?
No yearning in your inhibited soul?"
Puck was asked by the free roaming monkey bunch.
"Don't you have about liberty a hunch?"

Puck shook his head. "All I hear of is killing and war
Animals are tormented more and more."
With gusto a banana he peeled.
Happily on a swing he kneeled.
"We can roam around or go to sleep,
At all times the advantage of choice we reap."

While the exchange of words went on
A caregiver entered the cage with a ton.
He refreshed the water and cleaned the floor.
Sent the ape a smile then, with a bang, shut the door.
"You animals for sure have a good life
For comfort like this I always do strive."

Aha, Puck thought.
If a human would like to change with me
No need for a different environment I see.
The group of wild monkeys went away
Gone was their desire near the captive to stay.
Being monkeys they had problems to understand
What with the saying "To each his own" is meant.

In Africa

The baboon snatched my blonde wig and left me unkempt. I could not reach the monkey and retrieve my wig. On afterthought, I was lucky it had been a wig and not my own hair he had pulled.

Another First

I was on my lunch break and sat down on a bench to enjoy the first springy sun rays. It was May 1984 at Kennedy Airport in New York City. The bench was an old airplane-seating, two abreast. The maroon plastic was torn by wind, battered and faded by rain. It was propped up securely against the windowless wall of the airplane hangar.

I had spent 25 years as a stewardess. It was sad to see a 707 aircraft stripped down to the bare metal with the engine removed. The fuselage was standing across the field, no longer wanted by anybody. This reminded me of the days in 1959 when I had flown one of these birds on its maiden voyage across the Atlantic Ocean.

Progress? Good old times? Which is it? Now was the time of jet planes. Long gone was the DC-4, a four-engine propeller plane on which I had started my career in 1958 in the Inter-German Service of Pan American. Gone was the Stratocruiser with its luxury of bunks and staterooms, the plane which we had called the "pregnant oyster."

Many times during those years, I had served the then-president of Pan American Mr. Juan Trippe. He commuted on the Stratocruiser from his home in Bermuda to New York's JFK. As for the Stratocruiser, BDA-JFK was its final route before going out of service.

In 1960, my life became heavily influenced by Mr. Trippe. I had met and was dating a good-looking male flight attendant. At that time, the airline had a rule against flight attendants being married to each other. For that reason, marriage had not even become a consideration during our courtship. My beau was an outstanding purser and thus often assigned to fly on the Bermuda flights when Mr. Trippe was onboard. Other married couples who I remember and who benefitted from this were the O'Keefes, Ed and Betty Couto (our best friends) RIP, and the Pigmans.

One day Mr. Trippe asked, "How come a good-looking guy like you is not married?"

My friend laughed and answered, "Because I like my job and I am dating a stewardess. As you know, Pan Am will not allow married couples to fly for them. Neither one of us wants to give up flying."

President Trippe became serious, and his next sentence influenced the rest of my life. "We can change that. I will look into the matter and handle it. Go ahead and marry your sweetheart. You have my word."

So we became one of the first couples to get married and the rule was changed in 1960. Our honeymoon took us together on a working trip to Hong Kong. In 2010, we looked back on a 50-year marriage. It had survived even the existence of our great airline. ✈

Age Limit

I had just celebrated my 32nd birthday when the age limit for Flight Attendants was changed. The rule had been that you could only fly till the age of 32. The action was initiated by American Airlines.

Today there is no limit for the age of Flight Attendants. The oldest stewardess still flying with a commercial airline celebrated her 80th birthday in 2016. Bette Nash started flying for Eastern Airlines in 1957.

All that matters nowadays is a clean bill of health and a relatively attractive appearance. ✈

Rules Have Reason

While this story is fictional, this type of caper could easily have taken place in the life of a Stewardess.

Sandra heard the phone ring the minute she stepped into her apartment on Long Island. She dropped her suitcase and threw the blue uniform coat on the hook in the hall. The phone was standing on a little table and she got to it at the second ring.

"Long distance call from Istanbul. Hold the line please."

"From Istanbul?" Sandra's job as a stewardess had taught her to view many weird events as perfectly normal, but Istanbul?

"Hello, Sandra? This is Bob. How are you? I figured you would be home by now."

"Oh, it's you Bob! Yes, I just got in. We were rerouted to Washington yesterday."

"Sandra, did you mail the letter?'

Oh hell. The Letter! Bob had given her a letter to mail and it had completely slipped her mind.

"I told you I just got in. No, I still have the letter. You didn't tell me it is that important. Is that why you are calling?"

There was a pause at the other end. Sandra didn't remember giving her phone number to Bob.

"How did you get my phone number?"

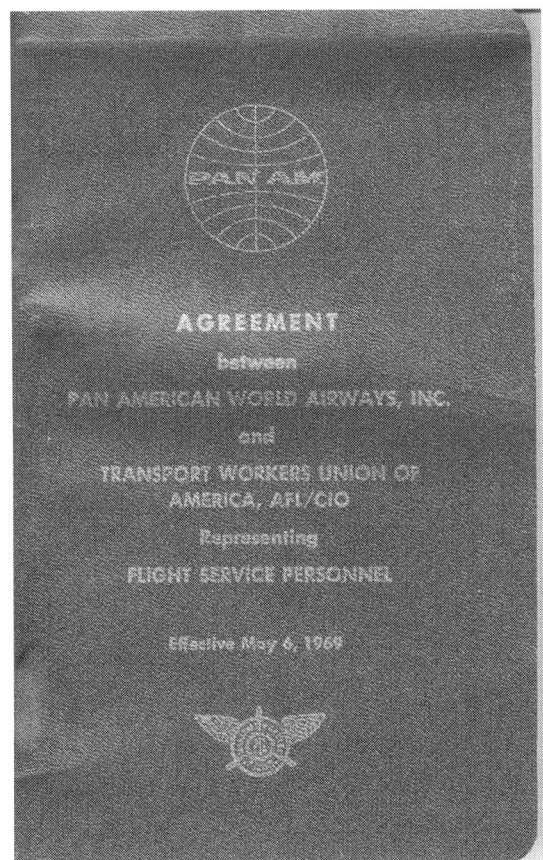

The pause continued, but she could hear Bob's breathing into the receiver.

"I inquired at your company," he finally said. And Sandra thought his voice to be somewhat agitated when he added, "Please do mail the letter today."

Then the tone of his voice changed back to the mellow, friendly tone by which she remembered Bob. "You know my uncle is so old, in his 80s, and tomorrow is his birthday. I really want to get my birthday wishes to him in time."

"OK, Bob, I'll drop it into the mail as soon as I get out of the uniform and into something comfortable."

"You are a doll. Drop me a note when you come to Istanbul again and I'll take you out to a real fancy place."

She ended the call with, "Thanks, take care." The connection went dead.

Sandra stared at her long, polished fingernails. Something did not sit right. She had met Bob only three days ago at the swimming pool of the layover hotel. A good-looking man, about 30 or so. According to him, he was American and working for some kind of U.S. outfit in Turkey. She had accepted an invitation to have dinner with him. He hadn't made any advances, just entertained her with charming conversation. He was an excellent dancer. They had agreed to meet again when she stopped over in Istanbul the next time.

Then the following morning he had met her in the lobby where she was waiting with her crew for pickup. He had taken her aside and asked her if she could mail a letter for him in New York – a letter to his uncle.

"You can't trust the mail here, and I want him to have it in time for his birthday."

She had agreed to take it, had put it into her purse and had actually forgotten about it till now.

Sandra kicked off her shoes and went over to the bar. She was not a drinker but enjoyed a cocktail here and there. She poured herself a vodka and went into the kitchen to add some ice and orange juice.

Why had Bob called her from Istanbul? She picked up the purse from the floor where she had dropped it. There was the letter addressed to a Walter Cropiat, 32 Brookstone Avenue, Bronx, NY.

If Bob had the money to call her about the letter, he should have called his uncle directly. On a hunch, she called information.

"Could you please give me the number for Walter Cropiat, 32 Brookstone Avenue, Bronx?"

"One moment please…sorry not listed."

Well, so much for that. A doubt had manifested itself in her mind. She could not shake the feeling that something was wrong. She should not have taken the letter in the first place. It was a company rule not to carry mail for anybody. She took the letter and held it up against the kitchen light. It was a plain white envelope. From what she could see, it looked like a note was inside with the white of the paper folded toward the outside.

Maybe I should just go and mail it and forget it, she thought to herself, but she did not move. She began to look through her own mail which had accumulated while she had been out on the trip. Bills, always bills.

In April, she would have her tenth anniversary with the airlines. The salary was good, especially when she picked up overtime but in the end there was never much money to spare. The rent, shoes on the Via Apia in Rome, dresses in Paris, and the luxury of a massage and hairdresser twice a week ate the earnings up in no time.

At 32, Sandra sometimes wondered about her future. She was not the Women's Lib type, but she had not yet found a man who impressed her enough to play house with. She had plenty of boyfriends and enjoyed meeting and dating men. Bob in Istanbul was one of them, the latest of her conquests.

The uneasy feeling returned the minute she thought of Bob and the letter. Suddenly she had an idea. What if she drove up to the Bronx tomorrow and delivered the letter to Bob's uncle?

It was a bright sunny morning when she woke up. She stretched comfortably. It was good to sleep in your own bed once in a while. Most hotel beds leave a lot to be desired. Today there was no rush to get up. This was the reward for the hectic life out on the line, with variable schedules, time changes, airplane reroutes and delays.

At 10 am she wandered from the bedroom to the bathroom and took a lukewarm bubble bath. The fragrance of Jean Naté added to her well-being. Maybe on the way back from the Bronx she could stop in Valley Stream and pay a visit to her Austrian friend Hans. He was a freelance writer and always ready to meet with her. Most of her friendships were like this. A sunny outgoing person herself, she had a flair for keeping friends. Sex was not always part of the deal. She played with open cards and made love when she felt like it, and she had never in her life hurt a friend intentionally.

The Bronx is not the greatest place to drive to but hopefully Bob's uncle lived in a relatively good neighborhood. She'd get gas and ask for directions once she got closer to the Bronx Borough. The drive was uneventful. Her old Ford did well. She had waited till after rush hour and it had worked. She drove over the Throgs Neck Bridge passing what had once been the amusement park Freedomland, and was now Co-op City. She was close to her destination. A few more miles. Okay. One more left turn and she had reached the address she was looking for. It was a four-story brick walk-up. More of the same right and left.

Just when she brought her car to a stop, she saw a black hearse pulling up. Her heartbeat accelerated. She remembered Bob saying, "My uncle is quite old. He leads a pretty boring life."

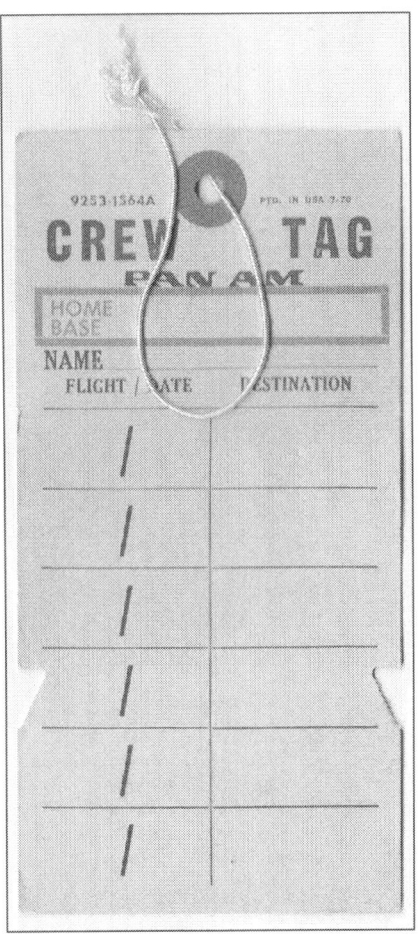

The address on the letter read Mr. Walter Cropiat, 32 Brookstone Avenue, 3rd Floor. It would be dreadful if the hearse had come to pick up the recipient of the letter. How should she handle that? She pulled the letter out of her Coach bag and gathering up her courage got out of the car and went over to the driver of the hearse.

"Excuse me. Could you tell me who died?"

The driver looked at her quizzically but obviously could not see a reason not to answer her. "It's a Miss Ralston. An old lady – 92 years old. I'm told she lived on the first floor."

Sandra felt relieved. So this had nothing to do with the uncle.

She went back into the car. She was going to wait till the hearse had finished his business. She did not want to have an encounter with a casket in the hallway of the house. Just as the hearse pulled away, she saw a police car stopping in front of her where the hearse had been. Two officers got out of the car.

"Was she in a no parking zone?" she wondered. One of the policemen went over to the building and stopped at the main entrance. He had his gun in hand. The other officer headed over in her direction. Sandra did not know what to make of that. The letter to Walter burned in her hand. She quickly crammed it back into her purse. Could the show of police have to do with that letter?

How could they know about her and the letter? The thought of dope smuggling had crossed her mind before. The uneasiness she'd felt because she had gotten herself involved now spread a paralyzing fear over her. The officer had reached her car waving his identification and motioning her to roll the window down.

"Madam, are you hear to see a Marco Rodrigo?" he asked.

"No. Who is Marco Rodrigo?" Sandra stammered. Her voice was so shaky and any color had left her face. She looked guilty, but the guilt came from carrying a strange letter and had nothing to do with that Marc or Marco. "Who is that Marco?" she ventured.

"A drug dealer we are here to arrest. But what are you doing here?"

The officer did not seem to believe her. Sandra quickly volunteered, "I have a letter for a Walter Cropiat from his nephew in Istanbul. It is Mr. Cropiat's birthday today. He lives on the third floor."

The other officer standing at the entrance to the building was getting impatient. He was waving for his teammate to join him. Sandra was praying silently that the officer would not ask what was in the letter. He would never believe if she said that she did not know. "Stay here," the officer said, "while we make the arrest." All the while he was copying her license plate number and make of the car. "We'll get back to you shortly." Obviously her demeanor had made him even more suspicious. She nodded and locked the car from the inside. So now she was becoming witness to a drug raid. It had been a nice but illegal gesture to accept the letter to bring it

from Istanbul to New York, a closed letter nonetheless. Damn it. Now, it was high-time to open it. She had to see what was in it. If there was something bad inside like cocaine or heroin at least the police would be back in a minute. A note fell out of the letter. It read:

Dearest Uncle,

Hope you get these birthday wishes in time. You always said I could do nothing in time. Hope this gets to you exactly on your birthday. I love you very much. Happy Birthday Uncle Walter.

Forever yours,

Bob

Sandra shook her head and giggled. Such an innocent note. The rush had truly been because Uncle Walter always reprimanded Bob for being late with everything.

About ten minutes had passed when the two policemen came back out of the house, a young guy in handcuffs between them. They dumped him into the police car and the officer Sandra had spoken with before came back over to her. By now Sandra was her good old self again and had no problem explaining who she was here to see and why. After they let her go, she went to see Uncle Walter, a nice old man she decided.

On her drive home, Sandra thanked her lucky stars that all had gone so well after all. Never again would she be a voluntary mail carrier! There are reasons why rules exist. ✈

Istanbul Airport

The manifest shows 244 overbooked passengers. Ground personnel is panicking. Great excitement till the reason is detected.

The names of the passengers were too long for the handwritten manifest form and each passenger name indicated two different people.

the last day of vacation

ALEXANDRA H. RODRIGUES
NYC

Every day, when listening to the radio, you heard your song; the theme about Pan American's stewardesses from all over the world and all the places to go. But while hearing it, you sat comfortably back in the velvet armchair, a cocktail in your hand and a grin on your face. Fleeting visions of your co-workers in the middle of a meal service on a full load, or circling over the New York area, made you even more relaxed.

But now the last day of your vacation is here. You wish it was the first again, for you can think of myriads of ways to spend another 30 days at your leisure.

Better go up to the closet and get your suitcase; you meant to have it repaired but never got around to it. What do they wear now, black or white gloves? Why bother looking into the manual, might as well take a pair of each. Where did you put the blouses? They are under a load of other garments because, when you started vacation, the time you would need them again seemed far off. And, oh yes, the uniform skirt, better try it! Those pounds that creep up during a holiday are with you this year too. Well, might as well go out and buy a real tight girdle!

Now the briefcase. Oh, what a mess! Aspirins, toothbrushes without covers, loose foreign coins, torn playing cards, your smock with gravy stains and those worn-out galley shoes, it is all there!

Back to the blouses, the buttons for them must be in a little green purse, but where is that purse?

Finally, you have recovered all the missing items and you slip into your uniform for a rehearsal. You pose in front of the mirror. You look great! That new pastel-pink lipstick sets off your brown complexion just right. But, oh shame, it is not regulation. You love the way your hair looks. Streaked from the sun and down to the shoulders, real feminine. But again, it won't make the briefing office, you still have to have it cut and tinted tomorrow.

The telephone rings, you are invited to a swinging party on Thursday. Lovely! But no, you won't be home. When this party probably reaches its peak, you'll be cleaning up the galley on a charter flight from Paris to Chicago.

Even so — you mean to buy perfume and lingerie in Paris and you'll call Pierre that nice man you met two months ago. You'll have room service again and sleep for 16 hours if you want to. Slowly the spirit for flying is returning and flashes a smile on your face. The stewardess smile.

3,000 Letters

These excerpts are from 3,000 or more letters I wrote to my mother during my flight career. She kept them by date in three consecutive folders. Marked "Alexa First 10,000 Words," "Alexa Second 10,000 words," and "Alexa Third 10,000 words." This idea had originated from the fact that I studied English with Langenscheidt's first and second thousand words of English. You see, I always planned to write a book. Out of my letters, I selected notes that will shine some additional light on my time with the airlines and my time in the United States.

April 4, 1969

I had written from Nassau in the Bahamas but then we could not get any stamps. The guy at the reception directed us to another desk. At that desk there was nobody at all. It was impossible to get any assistance. The public was in uproar because the flights were overbooked. The same commotion took place each year around Easter time. 50,000 people want to leave New York. And another 50,000 want to go to New York. For us that means lots of work.

April 5, 1969

Today we had off, and tomorrow we are flying to St. Croix. We need to be at the airport at 8 o'clock and will not get home till nine o'clock at night. Happy Easter.

Nassau is nothing special. An island somewhat larger than Bermuda but not as nicely taken care of. Loads of black beach boys who try to catch the Jewish schoolgirls. One also tried to get friendly with me. "Hello doll. Do you like it here?" I did not answer but could not get rid of him for a while. Ray was sitting a few hundred meters away in the shade. He watched us and laughed to himself.

It looks like there will be a strike on the 16th at midnight. We took already our money from the credit union so that we won't starve. If we didn't have to take it the boat would be paid by now, but things always turn out differently than expected.

Presently, we only have idiots as passengers. Constantly nouveau riche monkeys for which one cannot do anything right. However, we must stay polite and then to top it we need to say "thank you" to them at the end of the flight.

As an example, one wanted his steak real raw. I brought it to him and he complained it is cold. I offered to put it back into the oven and he answered, "Well then it won't be raw." What can I do in a case like that? He had given himself the correct answer.

When we were delayed out of NY, one guy takes his baggage out of the overhead and wants to get off the plane because he knew that at BOAC airplanes leave ahead of time. I opened the door for him, explained to the ground personnel that this man wants to get off, then closed the door, and we departed. However, all along I knew that BOAC was on strike meaning they don't fly at all. But the passenger was so disgusting that I was happy to get rid of him, and I helped him to get off. He'll be surprised when he finds no plane for him.

In addition, we had again a few cases when Ray had to give oxygen. Then he is fully occupied, and we poor girls have to do all the other cabin functions. Yes, a lot is going on. Other than the lack of money I would like a strike quite well. We could use some time to rest.

Nothing happened with the new uniforms. I did not even have a second fitting yet. But we do already have the hats which I find quite pretty and the new purse which

My husband Ray among others.

this time around at least is big enough and made out of leather. But the blouses are so narrow in the shoulders that I had to get a bigger size to be able to move in it. Now they wobble around the waistline. The shoes too are a problem. They cost $22 and are only available by catalog. How can one wear shoes without trying them on. Sometimes I have the feeling I'm working for an airline which is just beginning to exist.

I had written you that in Keflavik I bought a red leather coat with lamb lining. Very nice and good fitting.

On Monday Ray has to run around the airport with a sign in order to picket. I'm not going. Just what I need. Our union does nothing for us. But on the other hand, none of the young girls are interested in what the working conditions will be in five years. The average time as flight attendant is about 3 years.

On the Island flights we serve nowadays only California wines. That's not good for our wine cellar at home. It does not pay to bring wine home from the airplane.

April 9, 1969

They managed to assign Ray and I Pan Am's longest flight. Five o'clock in the morning we fly with Eastern Airlines to Boston. At 11 pm from Boston to Santa Maria to Lisbon and Rabat. Then we will have 3 days free in Rabat. Next day we continue from Rabat to Lagos to Johannesburg which is a 14-hour flight and the following day back the same way. Again 3 days free in Rabat, followed by our return flight to NY. It is a flight which we wanted to have for a long time already but never got. We stayed in the Hilton Hotel in Morocco.

Today my poem about the Pan American Stewardess was printed. I got it today and will send it to you.

(Dear Reader, You may view the Pan Am Stewardess poem on the back cover of this book.)

April 11, 1969

Tomorrow we have a nasty flight. Four hours with all the coffee pickers to Santo Domingo. Three hours there on the ground and then four hours back again. In addition,

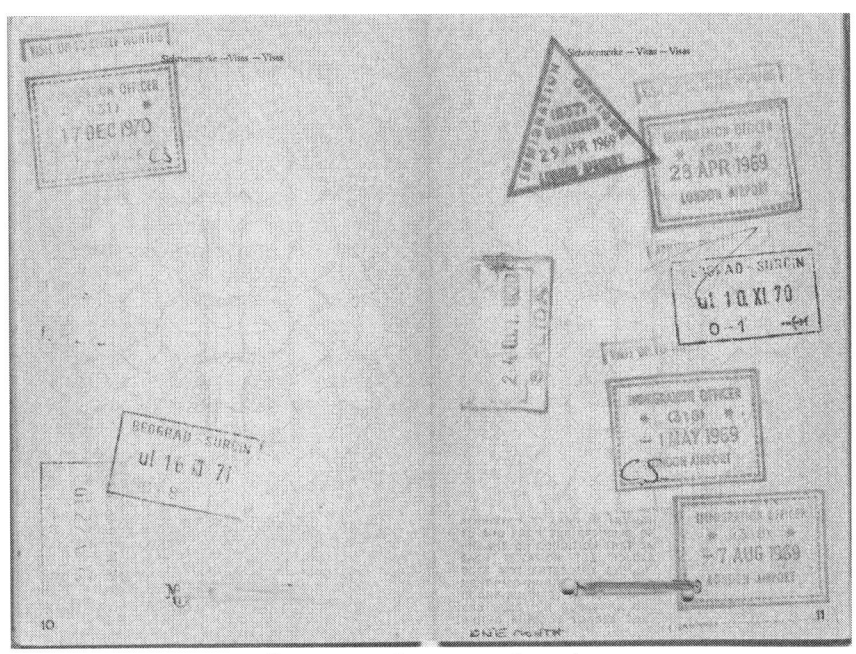
Our passports were well used.

our pilots are on a slowdown. Many purposely initiated delays. Does not do the cabin crew any good. We get paid 50 cents an hour for that.

Now it remains questionable if we come to Scotland.

Why does one have to be old to wear pearls? Most of our chicks, the new girls at Pan Am, fly to Tokyo and first and foremost buy themselves a pearl necklace. And then wear them all the time. Pearls are my birthstone (well, not stone really). I never am sure if I should by some. You can lend me yours.

The lessons for my writing class are getting harder and harder. But I do enjoy it. Every time I see a good story in a magazine, I think I could have done that too. So far, it is just in thought. Guess the muse has not yet kissed me sufficiently.

Already another plane was hijacked to Cuba.

We had a problem on our last flight. A woman with a baby and four dogs, first class, complained that nobody was helping her. We were very polite, helped her and calmed her down. Then shortly before arriving in New York, she told us that seven years ago she herself flew for five years as stewardess for Pan American. That sure took the cake.

On long flights we now have a coordinator. These are young men out of the hotel industry who are meant to organize the flight. That is because of the 747 airplane. Also there is a rumor that PAA wants to get rid of the male cabin attendants. In that case it would mean that they would have pay Ray one year's salary to make him quit. Ray says all that is nonsense, but I am not sure.

Well, with $10,000 we could certainly start something new. I would rather see that they pay me the money. I would immediately quit and write a long story about the unfairness at Pan Am.

April 17, 1969

We are home for three days. Our flight to Barbados which we had on our schedule was cancelled. They wanted to give a substitute of flying to Porto Spain but we refused politely.

Pan American was again in Cuba. We will find out tomorrow if we will come to Scotland or will have to demonstrate with signs at the airport, due to a pending strike.

Where do the Berlin stewardess's buy their shoes? Send me some. I still have not found any here in New York. I'm too lazy to go into the City to spend $22. The new date for the new uniforms is May 1 but I still have not had a fitting.

On my flight to Santa Domingo, I had a well-known fashion designer — forgot the name already. My little girls (stewardesses) always try to get his attention. The only one he talked to was a *bonita* Rodrigues. Do you know who that is?

I never throw your letters out. I have a suitcase in the attic. Would you like to buy them back?

April 19, 1969 New Coral Island Hotel Bermuda

This morning at 9 we were at the airport. Fog, thunderstorms, no airplanes, but many disgusted passengers. At 3 we finally left; 20 minutes out of NY we ended up in a huge thunder cloud and engine number four quit. No meal service for the passengers because the airport kitchen was standing under water. From 6 till 10 we sat at the airport in Bermuda, sipped on a coke and waited that the airplane should be repaired. Nothing. Now it is 11:30 at night, and we are finally in a hotel. They told us we will be called at 7:30 in the morning.

At the strike mediations, not much good happens. The mechanics and the workers and maintenance did again get the best deal. We did not get any numbers yet. If this continues, Ray will end up becoming a union boss.

Monday we are off. Tuesday they can give us another flight. We would like to stay at home. No way can we make up for the lost flight time which means a $200 deficit for us.

June 1969

On the 10th we are flying again to Hong Kong and on the 11th we will be in London so I will celebrate my birthday in London. We will be for two full weeks on the go. On the 22nd we come back from Hong Kong and 28th we have a charter to FRA, then via Swissair to Zurich. For me the first time in Switzerland apart from our short transit at the airport. Do you remember?

On the first of July we have a charter back to New York. Obviously we will make a lot of overtime this month. We will fly a total of 102 hours in June, and all my money that I spent in Hong Kong is easily coming back to me. You see, Ray doesn't complain. It takes quite a bit to fly that much when one hates flying.

In the Orient, monsoon storms all over, and we constantly are flying through heavy thunderstorms. My poor nerves. My guardian angel has plenty to do nowadays.

Today my right arm is hurting a lot. Had to get vaccinations for Cholera and Typhus. Plus, I'm still tired from the last flight and possibly also have a bladder inflammation because I sat at the Beirut pool for hours in a wet bikini.

It was 110 degrees in Thailand. This time we are flying London-Beirut-Delhi-Hong Kong and the same way back. Luckily we only have a short transit in Bangkok.

June 12, 1969

Ten o'clock at night. I am extremely tired. Now I am sitting in the cafeteria of the Kensington Hotel in London. Have suddenly gotten very hungry. Too long a wait for breakfast.

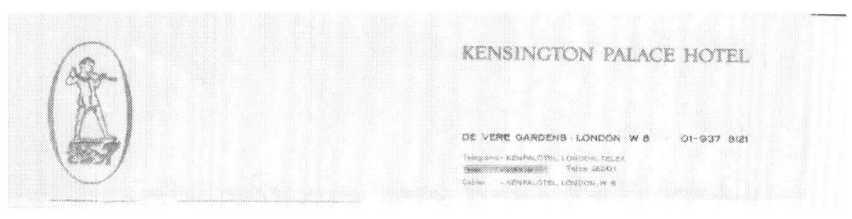

It is complicated to call Berlin from the Frankfort Airport. The aircraft is always parked far from the terminal. Our transit time is 30 minutes, out of which we wait 29 minutes for transportation.

I am sending you enclosed two pictures of our new uniform. Did you know we now have black girls flying for Pan Am?

June 18, 1969 Oberoi Intercontinental

It's 3 o'clock at night and I'm sitting in the coffee shop. I ordered an egg salad sandwich and a cappuccino. In comparison to conditions on the street here in New Delhi, with beggars all over, Harlem is a Utopia. During the day it is again 118 degrees Fahrenheit, while the air conditioners in the rooms make it feel like winter.

Our flight is delayed, but at 2 o' clock I was suddenly wide awake and hungry. So I just got up. At 4:30 am we will be picked up here at the hotel. Our destination Bangkok and Hong Kong. As always, my first task in Hong Kong is to visit Melwani, the tailor for all Pan Am crews. I did not know that the *Elegant World* and *Madame* had become one magazine. Nothing but advertisement.

(We used to take fashion magazines like *Vogue* to Melwani. He would copy gowns priced at $400-plus and charge us about $60. As a matter of fact, Melwani made my wedding dress.)

I don't know why I notice so many Germans every place. Ten minutes ago, a young well-fed man came in and ordered fried eggs and milk. Now he is complaining that he has been waiting already 20 minutes. The Indian waiter hastily ran back into the kitchen and brought the eggs while the German man did not even manage a thank you. How can anyone at 3 o'clock in the morning expect quick service?

Under my feet a little busboy in a mouse grey suit is cleaning the area. He is so agile in his movements that at first I did not even notice him. It is quite dark in here. Only two copper lamps are burning. I see the German guy getting up and leaving. I am sure he didn't leave a tip. I can hear the waiters complaining. The sounds of disappointment are the same in every language.

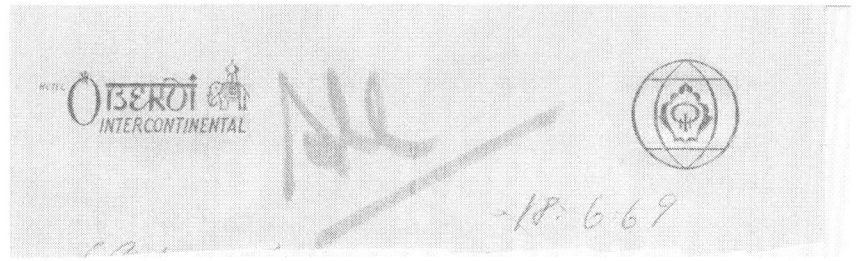

By the way, the flight from London to Frankfurt was delayed two hours.

Pan Am stocks are still falling. It is rumored that we had 40 million fewer passengers than last year. I would like to know why they plan on bigger and bigger airplanes all the time.

Now another guy is washing the floor with a mop that looks like a hairpiece.

June 30, 1969 Hotel Eden AU LAC Zurich

Nobody knew we were coming. Could not reach anyone at PAA. So we decided to look for a hotel on our own. Here we are now, Hotel Eden. "Au Lac" means at the lake. It is the Zurich lake, which was crowded like The Wannsee in Berlin during high season. We went to sleep right away and did not get up till dinner.

The air here is great, have all windows open. Our charter leaves this evening — all Jehovah Witnesses from Austria and Switzerland. They come to a main meeting in the Yankee Stadium on July 7 in New York.

Very high prices for everything here in Switzerland. A double room at least $30.- Dinner or Lunch for one person $8. Ten minutes Taxi ride $6.

(Funny what one used to call high)

This room has a funny balcony. You need to climb up to the height of the windowsill. That is where the entrance is. A nice big place with room for a table and two chairs. Weird. Guess they want us to get practice for mountain climbing.

July 1969 – Hong Kong

In another two hours we have to leave jewelry paradise. I bought an opal for $45 – green and blue, double layers and flat, set in gold. But I am still more interested in the one for $200, the one with the diamonds. I know that your opal has several layers. Here you can only find them with two or three layers the most. They are called black double opals.

Would be interested for how much this appraises in Berlin! I'll check it out in New York. From FRA I'll send you a pink coral stone. Paid $4 for it. I could get more like that even better in color. In addition, I bought a go-go watch for $2, two pairs of sunglasses at $3 each, and several blouses.

In Bangkok, I'll go for massage or rather have someone come up to the room. The locals are small people, and barefoot they will step onto one's back and massage it with their feet. Once you accept the oddity, it feels quite good. A manicure and pedicure ends the layover. Out of New Delhi to Beirut, we will wear the new uniform.

They sell great wigs here – real hair. Only $12, but it is not permitted to import Chinese hair into the United

States. Just heard on Radio Hong Kong, that the German mark will not be revalued – what a shame!

November 1967 Turnberry Hotel Ayrshire, Scotland

My eyes burn. Did too much reading. We still have another day here and tomorrow we go back to New York. Next week I will call you from Frankfurt – this hotel has an indoor swimming pool. The water does not look too inviting, but I will take a dip tomorrow before I go to the hairdresser.

The Tempelhof Airport was closed yesterday after we left. Later on they closed Tegel, too. We've been lucky to land. The return flight was not any better. The seatbelt sign was on all the way.

Right now we are drinking a Henkell Piccolo from the airplane. I put it a while ago on the windowsill to get nice and cold. Yes, cold weather can have its advantages like chilling Champagne.

November 17, 1969

Mom, it is your fault because you did not want to come to Paris. Now we have a problem. We missed our flight this evening because we misread the schedule and thought it meant tomorrow. We were just sitting with a bottle of Liebfraumilch and salmon, when Pan Am called to tell us this bad news. Now we are on call. Tomorrow between two and four we will find out more. This also spoils our flight schedule for November and most likely December. Also we will be separated and can end up any place.

(By the way, my husband and I flew most of the time together. We made a point to tell that we are together 24 hours a day. And that was the truth. Few people can say that.)

Later today we will watch the moon landing. Many people have lost interest in it as it is already the second time around.

November 30, 1969

Tuesday and Wednesday, we had 747 Boeing training. Thursday morning, we fly to Rome. Friday, I will call you from Paris. On every flight, I could let passengers be removed from the plane for making controversial remarks, but not those who make silly remarks are the dangerous one. It is the ones that act nice and politely one should watch out for.

September 1, 1973

Things look shaky at Pan Am. A lot of talk about Chapter 11, but that is not going to happen.

(Well it did happen, but much later).

November 1980

Not a great time at Pan American. Yesterday was the last work day for 295 flight attendants. A dinner for them in New York, and I had to hand them their final paychecks. I also had to ensure that they have no outstanding debits to the company.

On Thursday I had 80 people in my little office. Yesterday we had more than a hundred. The rest I expect on Monday. The atmosphere is depressing. The work hard.

(This was when I worked temporarily in management.)

December 1980

They cancelled a 26-hour flight on Ray's schedule – Dhahran Saudi Arabia in December. And now he is on call. It is hard to tell what is going to happen for Christmas.

We don't know what will happen at Christmas. We continue to plan to come to you at New Years.

Everything about Pan Am is in bad shape. They have lost $35 million in the last couple of months. In January, 30 percent more people will lose their jobs. I guess I will have to return to flight service. About my job in the City for Pan Am, I have not heard anything lately other than that I was released from there in good-standing. Weird how they do that here. From one day to the other one doesn't know what is happening.

Ray will be on the 6th and on the 13th in London. We now have a new layover hotel there – the Sheraton Hotel in New Hyde Park.

January 6, 1981

I'm back flying. The mood here is not great and everybody is waiting to see what the new organization will bring.

February 18, 1981

Of course I have been many times in Tokyo. We used to fly over Fairbanks, Alaska. Lately a direct flight of 13 hours has been introduced.

February 23, 1981

Now we have to wait to see how everything will go under President Reagan. He at least has humor and I like him quite well. In March, Ray flies four times to Rome and in February to Los Angeles.

February 27, 1981

Just now Danny O'Keefe came by with his wife. He is the purser who at my 30th Birthday party in the Bronx got himself totally drunk. Now he is on the wagon. He is on pension and looks small and shrunken. One can see how the years go by. Dagny, his wife who had talked with you in German, is still flying and has not changed too much.

March 27 1981

Tomorrow Ray is again going to Rome. The dollar is getting better and better. And I still have a lot of D-marks.

November 13, 1981

I finished my course in public speaking with Pan Am in Manhattan. ✈

Excerpts from a Flight Attendant's Diary

Assembled July 2012 from a diary beginning January 1970.

And then Alexa began to copy her diary from 1970. Paris – Rome. Arrived in Rome one hour past midnight. Airport deserted. Had sat in the cockpit most of the flight.

Temperature in Paris was 26° F. Rome 56° F. Snow, rain and thunder showers everywhere.

January 2, 1970 – The Fishermen's restaurant El Grotto, a favorite crew hangout was closed and we went to the place next door. As expensive but not as good as El Grotto. Had too much wine and too much cognac and coffee.

Met Dorothea an ex-stewardess and roommate of mine in Paris and had to listen for the hundredth time to her wondrous enjoyment and enchantment with her daughter Bettina. She forgot that during the same evening she had commented, "You're never yourself anymore." And "It is sure a sacrifice to have and raise a child." Rene, her husband, had fallen asleep in the hotel lobby, and I wanted to fall asleep too.

January 3 – But no sleep apart from a nightmare lasting a few minutes. Nauseous, dizzy, my eyes burned so that I had to brace myself against the stinging when I tried to force them open. Was afraid I might faint or throw up on the crew bus.

Full load because Air France was on strike. The hard work made me forget my aches and pains. Back in New York, my throat and bronchial tubes acted up, however the exhaustion let me sleep.

January 5 – Woke up with lots of energy to spare. During the day, spirits dampened by coughing spells. Snow is forecast for Wednesday. Wonder if I will make the next flight. Put on weight. Pan Am sent me a letter to come in for a weight check. Started to cough again and became grouchy with myself and Ray. Read Steinbeck's "The Pastures of Heaven." Don't like

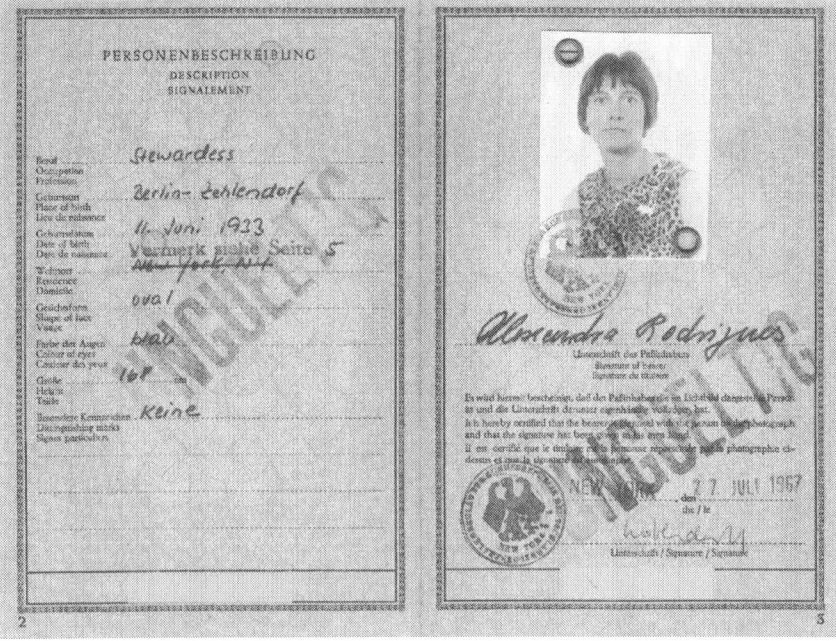

such collection of abnormal people. What is right and what is wrong? How valid are the standards by which we judge?

January 9 – Bought two dresses at Nina's boutique in Rome and walked around for nearly two hours, followed by a tall mean-looking guy. Dinner with the crew at Sciglio. Talk about sex becomes more permissible every day. Although many people harp on the behavior of the new generation, they indulge lustily in the subject of obscenity. Singing waiters, huge paintings, fishnets, but food like in an American diner. Ray had more than his share of wine.

January 10 – Captain Morris, Rome – Paris. Could not see even a smidgen of the Alps because of low cloud cover. Ordered delicious ham and cheese sandwiches despite trying to diet. Crispy French bread with the smell like coming fresh out of the oven. Ray is searching Pairs for cough drops as my cold is still hanging on. French police are stationed all along the hotel site. Seems they are expecting some riot.

We had a bite on the Rue Madelaine a place we knew from the times when the layover hotel was the Hotel de Paris, which has now become residential.

Paris streets are crowded with hippies. Men in ragged fur jackets. Girls in maxis or minis.

January 11 — Great flight back home. Had Emilio Pucci, the designer, on board. He appeared starved for recognition. Wanted to hold my hands and gave me some of his perfume. Stated that he believes in astrology and that Geminis (like me) are destructive. Has problems with people born under Libra. Took Pervitin during the War while flying missions, but does not believe in stimulants.

(During World War II, methamphetamine was sold in tablet form under the brand name Pervitin, produced by the Berlin-based Temmler pharmaceutical company – Wikipedia.)

Listened to the life story of a passenger by the name of Beer, who is a banker and appeared very immature, a name dropper. I was invited to have dinner with him and his wife in Paris.

January 12 — Got up early and tried to reach the flight service office to turn in my weight check. New snow is falling but not sparkling. Got an assignment back from the Writer's School — B minus. Did not expect any better. Will have to work with more discipline, so that the $800 tuition might eventually pay for itself. My best ideas come just before I fall asleep, but I do not write them down and on the next days they are gone.

First 747 flew to London yesterday and was already grounded with an engine change. Commercial flights with this aircraft will start January 21 on a daily basis.

January 16 – After a bumpy flight we are back in Rome. Garbage all over the streets. Subloads* on the plane who acted bossy and like a bunch of demanding spies.

(Subloads are airline employees or others flying on reduced fares.)

January 17 – Slept till five in the afternoon since our arrival in Rome and then went to a hairdresser who does not know much about his craft but it still beats my own styling. At night we went to a trattoria where we had some wine, cappuccino and dinner. It felt like spring. One did not need a coat and the air was still, which does not contribute to healthy sleep without a breeze. The rooms in the Hotel Metropole unfortunately are small, smelly and overheated. Traffic in the city is obnoxious.

January 18 – Rome to Tehran. Good flight. Light load. Crew party. Uneventful layover.

January 21 — FCO/JFK Captain Emmens. Smooth flight, but empty and boring. Passed the time with crossword puzzles and word games.

Sil Broglia, a supervisor, called. Jobs for in-flight directors are being offered to male pursers. This might bring our happy flying-together career to an end. Ray and I both smell a rat. The first commercial flight of the 747 was delayed today for 6 hours because of an overheated engine. They had to change aircraft. PAA is getting one black eye after the other and passes it on to its workers: us.

January 20 — Rome had nice sunny skies but we stayed in the room after we arrived from Tehran, played cards and then went back to sleep.

Royal Tehran Hilton
TEHRAN, IRAN

January 22 — Had a light dinner at not especially good trattoria and went to bed early. The Italians are quite unfriendly lately. Probably because the country is getting too much tourism and turning into a second France.

Tehran. An anemic sun shines on sand-colored houses. The background is surrounded by haze-covered mountains. A glare comes from the sparsely snow-covered peaks. One misses color. A piano player evokes memories of 15 years ago, the time in Germany

> ### THR Tehran
>
> Our layovers in Tehran capital of Iran were never very exciting. Even in the 1960s, a political doom was apparent. Besides hanging out by the pool, the highlight of the day was a trip out to eat. That required getting a cab. Taxis were not plentiful, but cab drivers were interested in foreign girls, preferably blondes. My husband and I had worked out a plan that never failed. Let me clarify: I was a blonde or was sporting a blonde wig at that time. My husband would let me stand at the curb for a taxi while he was hiding further down the street. When the cab stopped to pick me up – which happened every time – I would get in the cab. Then my husband magically would appear and get in also. This to the great dismay of the cab driver. So we always got our cab.

which I closed like a read book behind me, yet never will forget.

January 22 – Ray went to Pan Am for the director interview. I'll try to put a little order into the house, which as usual the day after our arrival looks like hell. Could this be the beginning of the end? One day

I will have to quit. Well, no use worrying about this now. President Nixon's speech was nothing but a diplomatic farce. The stock market dropped right afterwards.

January 26 — Another moronic conversation with Sil Broglia about my weight check. Sil is one of the Supervisors for the Flight personnel.

(By now he is dead and my weight, which at that time was 134 pounds, 130 the limit for my height.)

Flight 114 JFK-ORLY. Three pounds above my established weight could put me on an unpaid leave of absence. Three occurrences like this could put one's job in danger. All the supervisors in the office are obviously in competition with each other, and to let out steam they pick on the girls. Unfruitful competition is what destroys this company.

On the flight, Arthur Goldberg (who had served as U.S. Supreme Court Justice and U.N. Ambassador) and wife, the President of Christian Dior Furs, and very upset and very snappy PAA captain in first class on vacation.

January 27 — Waiting far too long for our bags at Paris customs. Passengers begin to grumble. Pain in my feet. A party in the Grotto made us decide to eat in the hotel. No atmosphere. Dreams are beneficial to

liven up some dull days. But keep your dreams to yourself. Once they break through the conscience, they are bound to hurt your best friends.

January 28 — ORY/FCO Captain Charles Morris very nice and kind of a lover boy. Heavy clouds over Rome but warm. 13 first class and 67 economy passengers.

FCO/ORY — Four First Class and 48 Economy

January 29 – Flight 114 delayed. I'm already in uniform but we are now left with two more hours till pickup. Probably a mechanical. It is that lemon plane 706 on which just about nothing works.

January 30 – Success. Went for weight check and scale showed 128 pounds. Good.

February 1 — An ambassador had left an expensive gold watch on the plane, and it was given to me to bring to London traffic control office on Flight 100. We had terrible turbulence on approaching Heathrow Airport. Flying through one heavy, fast moving rain cloud, which took over 5 minutes. Still very few people get as nervous in such a situation as I do.

February 3 — A peaceful day in Frankfurt. Followed my notion and became a redhead. Not sure now if I like it. Between Ray and me, we had 2 bottles of wine and I felt sick as a result. Blue sky changed to pouring rain at April speed and that in February

February 5 — Flight 1, London/NY. We had 25/81 passengers, worked hard and got many compliments. When we came home, the temperature in the house was 34° and all my beautiful plants, those lovely green foliage, which I had nursed over the years had their leaves hanging, dead and frozen. I felt like crying. A sadness overcame me, and the thought that people die in many places without cause or reason, prevented me from becoming hysterical about my plants. What about the idea of deep-freezing people for a future resurrection? It would not work on plants and thus I felt this project was further off than expected.

February 7 — We got interested in an ad we saw for a couple being sought to handle U.S. commissary in Moscow. Salary $7,500 and free accommodations. We certainly had the qualifications but what's the use of us down-stepping financially. It proves though that both of us are quite restless. We are both too intelligent and ambitious for PAA. We give them more then they give us, yet we have the ideal set-up by flying together. The shadow of the 747 hangs over our heads and it seems unavoidable that a change will come and not one for the better.

I don't think about age too often. Not like Olenka who is haunted by complexes and the fear of getting old — but how long can I stay a stewardess? Some of the newly hired girls could be my daughters, which is quite depressing. Yet it is great to be my age but not looking it and to be able to be fascinating and interesting.

(Now, in my 80s, I am thinking about age all the time. I just re-read the above and, oh well, since I wrote it, I have put on 55 pounds and cannot shed a single one. As to Olenka, our friendship had broken up a long time ago but oddly enough I just found out via computer that her husband Sverre, who she divorced when we had just met, died in 2010 and Olenka, herself now 89 years old, has an address in Great Neck Long Island. Possibly she is in a home.)

(The date is January 2, 2015. Three years have passed since I worked on that little diary. It has been here on my desk all along but has been ignored. Just looked up Emilio Pucci: 1914 – 1992. His fashions are still being offered in the high-fashion world.)

February 9 — JFK/STU. A 747 crew was in the briefing room. For next month everybody is bidding around that Jumbo. Nothing on it is yet organized and F/S is having a hard time on it. Two pursers were to be fired for stealing liquor money and sleeping on the plane, but both are now In-Flight Directors. The scum on top as always.

Stuttgart. At the hotel desk they tried to cheat me out of 1 Mark for magazines. No luck. Had venison for dinner. Stuttgart is the only place I can find it, and I do like the taste with lingonberries very much. The rooms were overheated, so we slept with the windows open, and I guess I got myself a cold from it.

Brussels. Large, colorless buildings and even our hotel with its huge chandeliers and imitation marble columns does not appeal to me. There is no gaiety. Brussels is civilized, clean and dull.

February 18 JFK/Shannon — Tremendously foggy and again three inches of snow with freezing rain.

Captain Schattenkirk is in command. He appeared stuck-up until I got him interested in doing the Sunday Times crossword puzzle with me. Only had 2 passengers, one of them an IGS (Inter German Service) pilot. Had a big backfiring at the landing in Shannon and the engines chewed up two birds. Joy looked pregnant to me. Her uniform skirt is tight, and she looks round all about her belly. A day of nothing, so typical for Limerick, Ireland, where we have our layover. A small boutique with outdated novelties, one radio station and a dusty lobby, a few British newspapers presented the entertainment. Our two girls are sad sacks, and this kind of entertainment must be the peak of luxury for them.

February 17 — Freezing at the hairdresser. The two beauticians had ice-cold hands but rosy cheeks, so typical for the Irish. Irish coffees are the only highlight of the Limerick cuisine. Although the food appears appetizing, it is absolutely tasteless. I am eating two meals a day and hopefully not overdoing it in calorie intake.

Nice lunch with Mirette Hanley.

(She later became Mirette Hanley-Corboy, known throughout Ireland for her contributions to construction, business and education.)

Good flight, beautifully smooth and not too many people, Ray suffered through it and felt better when we got to the Dollhouse.

(Dollhouse is what we called our residence in Massapequa, Long Island. It is the house where I still live today. At the time of this diary, it was a small ranch we had bought in 1964. Cute and on the water.)

February 24 Robertsfield, Monrovia — Arrived dead tired but still went to the pool for a couple of hours and now have the beginning of a sunburn.

Good flight back from Robertsfield on February 25. Joe Borgess was deadheading. We played chess and flirted as usual. People cannot understand how a marriage can remain pure and happy through nine years. They are the ones who never had the luck to experience the fine and intricate wave of really and truly sharing and loving. They are the ones that have flings without consequence.

For us, the model worked. Whet your appetite outside, but eat at home.

February 28 JFK/SNN — Uneventful. It was funny to meet Sydney Schroeder who was with us years ago on the foggy Washington drive with the sleeping driver. Heard that she is going to marry Jerry Cox, while I thought that he is infatuated with Marita Rostad, a Norwegian stewardess.

(She too is dead I believe but I do remember a joke that Ray always made when the talk came to her. "10,000 Swedes running thru the weeds, chased by one Norwegian.")

Went to see a movie "Mr. Cognac." An adorable film about a little poodle. The theatre was cold but the Irish are used to that. If it was hot they feel they would come home and catch a cold in their insufficiently heated apartments.

(The movie reminds me of our little, mean poodle. We called him Ego. He was white, small, had a pedigree and was as cute as he was mean. He would go after everyone's legs. Guess he had unfulfilled sex drive as is common with royalty. We had bought him in London from a lady who was breeding dogs, and Ego was the brother of another white malik who came to live with an actress. We got him for company to Ray's mother who lived in the same house with us. He sure gave us many problems. After Mom died, we had to bring him from Long Island, where we had moved to, all the way into the Bronx so that Ray's sister Irene could take care of him.)

March 2 – A trip to the Bronx to pick up a dirty and overgrown Ego. But oh was he happy to see us. He was panting terribly but as soon as we arrived in the Dollhouse the therapy of this place worked tricks. Irene got heavy and she knows it. She is in a rut and does not know how to help herself.

(Irene is now in her 80s. She moved to Colorado and is all alone. Her son Mark will not talk to her and we do not know why. She also has a grandson and granddaughter, both of them will not pick up the phone ever.)

Ray's older sister Sally has psychosomatic headaches and keeps her husband Curly busy.

(They both are dead too. So many people that built our life in the past by now are gone.)

Claire and Sam are the same pleasant old Jews. Was awoken by a call from Ann Decker. It seems that she was trying to get out of serving us dinner. Lee Roy, her husband, wanted to play tennis, which at a temperature of 34° with 30-mile winds, is idiotic. I said "'no?' but we will go tonight and play bridge with them. Ego decided to piss on the couch out of spite.

(Of course the memories are manifold. 42 years or more have gone by. Lifetimes for many people and the end of the line for many people I knew during this period of time. Each of these memories, a story of its own. As a Realtor, I sold Decker's house. Lee Roy ended up with Alzheimer's. Their son was a race driver. What happened to Ann I do not remember.)

Ann had made shrimps and we had an enjoyable evening. I like Lee Roy better than her. This is her second marriage. The two boys are from her first marriage.

March 4 — Met my mother in Berlin. It is so hard to share emotions during one hour of transit time. It would be easier to meet with a stranger instead of with a person one loves. Already before we get there I am aware that we will only have a limited time together before I have to leave again, and consequently my psychic self refuses to be itself. Still snow in Berlin and the airfield is guarded by soldiers with guns in case of an attack. So things have tightened since the Swissair crash.

Got together with Danny and Dagny. They are another married flight crew couple. They are old-timers and rather conceited, not quite our cup of tea. But it is fun to chat with them for a few hours.

(We never became true friends, like with Betty and Ed, but I will always remember the show that Danny O'Keefe exercised on Paulding Avenue in the Bronx, for my thirtieth birthday. He got terribly drunk and pulled, at that time, daring jokes. Later in time their daughter, a great swimmer, lost her life trying to help a friend. The rope of a boat strangled her or something to that respect. We felt so bad. Danny died a long time ago, not sure if Dagny is still alive.)

We walked through side streets of Limerick. Saw Quonset huts, burned out ones and some lived in. It shows the poverty is as much present in cultivated countries as in the under-developed regions. Dirty children and drunk old bums.

March 6 — SNN/JFK. Had a couple of passengers flirt with me again and lost 75 cents playing Gin Rummy. My neck hurt and I was glad to get home. After a few drinks and a talk at the kitchen table, I slowly began to relax.

March 14 — Out of JFK we had Captain Valentine, the husband of Jenny Roice. She is the one that hired me for Pan Am International. Out of Brussels, captain Emmons.

(February 27, 2015 — Got sidetracked. Another chapter has come to an end. My good friend, Ann Claps passed away on Sunday at the age of 97. Unfortunately, I have not seen her or been able to talk to her for many years as she was stricken by severe dementia since 2008. We were good friends. The first time I met her was when I was pregnant with my son Raymond. She then was a supervisor at Pan Am and I had gone in with my husband Ray to pick up some papers for a leave of absence. The time is close to the above happenings. We became true friends, family to family. Her husband Jerry was a treasure. He worked at the Pan Am Credit Union at JFK and he was always helpful and friendly. He passed away before Ann, when my husband was still alive. I will miss them both.)

March 14 — *The layover in Shannon was overshadowed by my mother's sickness. What a time she had chosen for moving. There is still snow in Berlin. Kurt has to do all the work. Wasn't even in the mood to call Irmchen or Marianne, despite that it was Sunday and calls are cheap.*

(Irmchen is my girlfriend and Marianne is the mother of my godchild. Both of them still alive! Hurrah. It is somehow depressing to only bring up memories in which the people I wrote about have passed on by now.)

March 15 — *The food and service at Vincent's lacked quality. We had to ask twice to get seconds of bread. It was raining and the bed's uncomfortable.*

March 16 — *Captain Valentine BRX/JFK. Had the counsel to the Congo Mission on board and made friends with him. He's putting us on the official reception list for the United Nations. I sure would like to attend one of those affairs and see those big bosses that run the country.*

March 22 — *JFK/BDA/JFK Got our lines for April. Jess and Edith were on edge when we played bridge. Edith is still very sensitive and Jess loves to rub it in. She didn't bring the NY Times puzzle. She's slipping. I wonder who their friends are or if they have any. Never see anybody there. Never anybody calls.*

April 11 — *JFK/BDA We've a very nice crew this month. Pretty girls. Likable and good workers. It's a* pleasure to work with a group like they are and incentive to do better oneself.

When in Boston ate at the Falstaff Room in the hotel — what a meal!

Six-dollar-fifty for a steak, and what a steak. A gourmet delight from the cheese dip to the crisp salad

and butter-soaked baked Idaho potatoes with sour cream and chives.

BOS/BDA/JFK Full loads but nice people and a smooth flight. No matter we were tired till we got back to the Dollhouse. Had as usual some drinks to relax and again we philosophized at the kitchen table. Who is to say that talk runs out after a few years of marriage? I should get back to my writing. What happened to all my enthusiasm? Laziness.

Lola, my gym teacher, said she would stop by to have some Champagne but maybe she thought I didn't really mean it because it's now 5 in the afternoon and she has not shown up. Here I went out of my way and spent $10 on cold cuts. I still seem to be too considerate always to people. But the rewards are minute.

Pan American called and changed our report time. Apollo 13 is in trouble. Everybody worries if they get back safely. They sure show stable nerves and calmness during the emergency.

JFK/HEL Pan American had changed the report time and when we got to the airport nobody knew about it making it a long night. Whereas the majority of the flight left me cold.

Was too lazy to get a sauna and massage, although this is the place for it, but my eyes bother me constantly so I spend most of the layovers sleeping. No use going out and getting a cold. It is still winter here. I could have bought some clay pots but we are deadheading and it is hardly worth to carry all that stuff.

April 13 — The Pan American drive toward better understanding is showing only very minute success. There seem to be few bosses around by now. Whenever I get really mad at them like after the one flight when a stupid survey took priority over any passenger needs, I claim that there are in Pan American thousands that work, hundreds that think, and only handful that work and think.

Ray is not going to the hospital till the beginning of our vacation in June. Since the doctor decided his hernia shouldn't be done yet. I am relieved that I don't have to fly alone. It's not the work or responsibility I'm afraid of, but truly the only way I can take the agony of flying is by having him around. All logic does not help. No passenger is ever half as scared as I am. Funnily enough, it has become a state of mind that enables me to relax completely once the airplane touches down. On April 20, we are going to deadhead back on the 747 which is going to be another challenge for my nerves. New airplanes are viewed by me with awe. It could be diagnosed as flying claustrophobia. Mr. Fabian the passenger I *played chess with called but twice I wasn't home so we had a bottle of champagne put on the flight for him and we are going to call him in Hamburg.*

April 18 — Still snow in Finland. The service at the restaurant awfully slow. To learn foreign languages comes easily to me. Finnish however is a language I could never pick up. The words are extremely long and seem never to end. FLT 75 HAM/AMS AMS/JFK CPN/AMS Bought fresh tulips in Amsterdam

A SHORT LAYOVER IN 2015

Risen

Spring 2015. There is still none of the silky, velvety touch in the breeze that one does expect at this time. It was a hard winter this year on Long Island and spring seems to be afraid to take over.

I pull into my driveway and get out of my by now already seven-year-old BMW.

My mind ponders about the passing of time and things. I grab my cane, a dancer once I now have problems walking.

Alongside the driveway and my neighbors' fence is a flower bed. It has been there ever since we bought the house in the

1960s. We were a young, freshly married couple, ready to live the American dream of being owners of a little house with a white picket fence. My husband Ray and I were then both flying as cabin attendants for the international airline, Pan American World Airways. "Gone but not forgotten" is the motto by which it is still remembered by many after going Chapter 11 in the late 1980s.

I notice that weeds gleefully try to take over, and an old lilac bush is laboring to produce bloom. It too was young and pretty once. It is here, and it is giving its best.

I startle – what is that? A flaming red, long stemmed, straight and lush tulip has caught my attention. Now memories overwhelm me. During the first years in our new house we had planted one hundred hand-picked tulip bulbs which we had personally selected in Amsterdam at one of their famous tulip fields. We had been on a layover on Flight 72 from Idlewild, now JFK, to Amsterdam and Berlin.

During the first and second year after we had planted the tulips, we were highly rewarded for our efforts. When those plants bloomed in the month of May, in multiple colors, proud, straight and in abundance they had been the talk of the neighborhood. With time, as the years went by, the display got less and less note-worthy.

Fast forward and only a few measly tulips stubbornly remained. Finally, after several Nor'easter storms, they all were gone. Now here it was, one survivor. Yes, I am sure it is a flower that has risen from the original crop. It has risen after having been buried for decades. Possibly it was pepped back to growth, when Super Storm Sandy caused the town to dig into this part of my yard. What a heartwarming moment. I quickly got my camera, took several pictures of that amazing flower and gratefully acknowledged the surprises that life sometimes has in store for us.

NOW BACK TO THE JOURNEY

April 19 — Sent my assignment to Famous Writers School. And also the data for the market research. Will either one of them become profitable?

April 21 — 747 Class Boeing Emergency training for Pan Am flight service which we had to undergo once every three months. A joke. Two hours of talk. A waste of time. But for a few hours we enjoyed the idea of getting four hours flight time paid for.

At 8:30 at night they will tell us about a pattern change. 20 hours flight time. Cannot see my mother in Hamburg. Time lost to reschedule. Seldom have I seen Ray so mad. It's a dirty trick but after taking it apart it seems we can do absolutely nothing about it except maybe bring attention to the attitude of scheduling.

April 22 — Captain Anders who hardly ever talks to you on a charter of radio and television executives.

153 women and one man. Worked out fine. Got an invitation to a reception with Princess Margaret but

of course one cannot bother Pan Am with such details.

Their talk about public relations is as cheap as all that sensitivity trend going on. Mr. Halaby proved that to me on the only flight on which he was my passenger. We have always remained a dispensable number.

(Najeeb Halaby served as CEO and chairman of Pan Am)

April 23 — Now we are in Rome after deadheading with Alitalia. I want to use the lavatory on the ground but the stewardess told me they have a regulation against it. After I explained that I am with Pan American and never had heard of such a thing, she got a little worried. I'm sure it's a rule she made up herself

Captain Kunter and the girls went into town shopping since we were staying at Fiumicino. Nothing works our way this time, and Ray and I are in a bad mood because of it.

To get the HAM flight is as big a chance as seeing an airplane ditch in a swimming pool. Charter ROM/BOS deadhead to LGA.

Eastern Airlines cancelled their shuttles because of NY weather. We went on Pan Am 115. I got hysterical. Worst flight I can remember. Big cumulus clouds full of electricity and we were in it for two hours. I got so scared I thought it was going to be all over. Landed in JFK with visibility less than 50 feet. Still feel shaky today but already got another flight for tomorrow night. How much worse can it get?

April 26 — At 11:40 pm we reported and ferried to Boston. A very noisy hotel. Captain George Pistol, a good sport and I know him from the IGS, had been to a flea market and picked up some nice planters.

Got a sunburn in the yard while potting cacti.

April 27 — BOS/STX/JFK The water around St. Croix was so calm it looked frozen. 80° and high humidity. St. Croix and St. Thomas don't look like anything. Smaller than Bermuda and barren. People spend good money to vacation here. For what? Got home at 2 am. We had 116 people in the economy section.

May 2 — Brought Ego back in to the filthy Bronx after a new breezy sunny cool day. Got many compliments for my suntan. Our girls this month are zombies, especially the redhead Colleen. She acts like a zombie smelling her fingers and staring around with bleary eyes. Conda is a new girl. Very young which accounts for her scatterbrain, but pleasant and pretty. Captain Scott is very nice. I was still scared after hearing about the DC-9 crash 35 miles off St. Croix in which 23 people died.

May 3 — Once again in the Turnberry Hotel in Ayrshire, Scotland. The guests are mostly older couples which makes us feel quite young. It is encouraging to see old people like this full of vitality playing golf and enjoying life. Not to forget that those people are financially well situated as otherwise could not afford a hotel like this. They all look as if they just came from a 1920 hairdresser. Clean, but old-fashioned. The evenings are long. At 8:00 you can still see golfers hit some balls.

May 4 — Three hours of shopping in Munich without buying anything worthwhile. The whole crew went to have dinner at the Mathäser (beer hall). Food was excellent. Joel had his wife along on the whole trip. He is very proud of her. They make a fine couple. Don't drink, don't smoke, but are game nevertheless. We played a couple of hands of bridge but there wasn't much zest in that.

May 5 — Ray went to play golf for five hours. They played 18 holes and came back completely exhausted. I took a bath and a nap, and it was a peaceful day. Finished up with another rather boring bridge game with Joel and Carolyn.

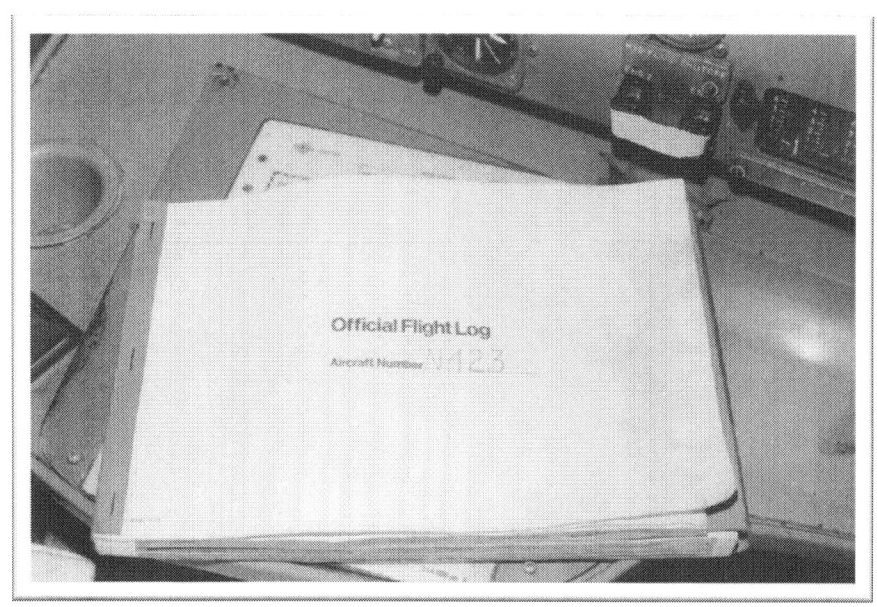

May 6 — It's impossible to make plans. At home we found a note changing Ray's operation to June 11. This gets me nervous because my mother is all set to come to NY on May 29. Our last flight before vacation. Ray caught a miserable cold. For the first time in years, he slept nearly through the entire flight. Luckily, it was an easy trip — hardly any passengers.

Captain Scott was a good sport. Always pleasant and my girls are bearable. Conda is cute, the exact image of Patty Duke on TV.

May 7 — A picturesque day. Clear blue sky. Lots of fire red tulips and young leaves in saturated green sprouting from lilacs and mountain ash. But once I put my nose out, the illusion broke. North winds at 50° made for a chilly day.

May 10 — Ingrid came to visit. She has learned a lot about Waldemar. He is good looking. A Polish Count and an expert in his engineering job. Obviously, he sees this as more than enough enrichment to his marriage. He's given up as far as Ingrid's flying goes. He likes his peace while she is away. A weird setup. No longer the big love. I'm sure it most likely never was, but possibly they make a go of it with both sides calming down.

May 12 — Alaska — What a surprise. The flight took us seven hours over Canada, all uninhabited areas. Lots of frozen lakes and rivers. Fairbanks is 140 miles south of the Arctic Circle and the temp was 70°. It is a quite primitive city with many interesting old log cabins. Saw only a few natives — that is Eskimos. Prices are twice as high as the other parts of the States. But I understand that salaries are quite good. A beer 90 cents. Dinner in the coffee shop 6 dollars. To rent a car for a day 18 dollars.

The Los Angeles palm tree is not too happy in Long Island climate and looks puny. The tulips have had it. This morning they had lost all their leaves and stems. All evenly long green stems. The lilac is out and smells of youth, spring and romance.

May 18 — JFK/SNN Captain Hunt. Rather empty plane and we are so lucky to still be away from the 747s.

Barbara ran away with Steve Angus. This is really a modern affair, Ray said. He could have knocked me over with a feather after Ed Riley told him the story. Barbara had been going with Stu for quite a while already. They sure did a good job in hiding it till now. It surprised even me. Two marriages both over 12 years broken up.

May 19 — Prague is colorless. The sign of a communist country. No drapes. No pictures. People are dressed in post-war clothing. Little to buy. The few things available like antiques are priced for tourists who are the only ones able to afford them. However, formalities have eased and one is free to venture through the city, take pictures and talk to people. Went to eat at a local place but being with the entire crew spoiled it. Furthermore, I was tired and depressed.

May 20 — Shannon once again. Had called my mother from Dusseldorf during transit. Our stay in Shannon is more cultivated than Prague. It has interesting pictures on the wall. Reminded me of Keats. The rooms are penthouse-like with slanted beamed ceilings. The Bunratty Castle is the place where tourists are said to gain the gift of gab. They are made to lean backwards out of a window while castle attendants hold their legs. For a fee, of course. Bought pretty colored crystal glasses in Prague. Had salami and gruyere cheese for breakfast.

May 23 — Picked up a cute blue coat for $25 at a Jewish bazaar rummage sale. Also bought a white purse for 24 cents and when I opened it at home found a 10-cent stamp in it. A petty thing but it made me feel good.

Black people pick up worn clothing by the carton and they push and pull with their elbows as if they were looking for real treasure.

May 24 — An antique show in Manhasset for the benefit of the North Shore Hospital. Loads of dealers displayed goods on car hoods, blankets and small tables. The prices asked for all items were outrageous. This got even Ray interested and it seems highly worthwhile to look into that kind of business somewhat closer. Maybe we can make our kind of job profitable after all.

May 25 — Now the Mercury 442 really broke down and it was very nice of the Reibers to drive us to the airport. Waited two hours on the runway for clearance. I had all subloads in First Class, and Captain Wise's daughter together with the grandmother annoyed me. A 15-year-old girl drinking Champagne and never saying please or thank you. But the flight went off smooth otherwise.

May 26 — Played poker. We are both tired and slept after we arrived for a few hours but not enough. We can still feel a sluggishness, and without enough sleep our ambition for anything always runs low.

May 27 — In Munich we went into a Meissen (porcelain) showplace. A new 18 piece set $400. A single old plate $100.

We ended up in a handicraft place buying modern but hand-painted goods for $43. Had white asparagus for dinner. Was delicious and by 10:00 we were asleep. Had called my mother.

May 28 — Scotland is as pretty as a picture. Clear blue sky and brisk wind with the scent of salty sea. Sheep still babies, only weeks old and now growing. Cows grazing on the hilly lawns among the heather bushes. Took a ride to Gerwin a lovely fishing town and watched weather-beaten fishermen unloading their prawn shrimp and flounder. Undisturbed by the nosey stares of dressed-up tourists like ourselves. Busses with American Express tours pass through the village frequently. Well, vacation has started but there is no elation because Ray's pending operation is spoiling the fun.

June 6 — Picked up my mother from JFK. She stayed up with us till 10 pm which is amazing after the miserable flight she had. She is happy to be here and will need some rest. Ray's operation is hanging like a cloud over us. He is so sweet and does not seem troubled at all, but there is a morbid atmosphere and

I am scared that something might happen to him. I love him so much and once more am acutely aware how dependent I am on him. He is working on the boat and is keeping busy. Probably in order not to think about the hospital. Here I have my mother and could keep her company, but I keep looking at Ray and already the tears are close and I have to wear sunglasses because sometimes I cannot suppress them.

How dreadful to bring Ray to the hospital. Right away they took tests and put a wristband on him, which made him the patient. I felt miserable all evening. f it wasn't for my mother, I would get hysterical. So I have to force myself to put up a front because I don't want to act silly, and silly it would be. The house is empty without my husband. The procedures have started and Ray looks pale. His voice is subdued and there is some kind of resignation about him. The hospital is nice. If one can say that about any place where people go only as a last resort. Luckily there is none of that smell so common in meat markets. The whole place is run efficiently — office-like. Ray has one roommate who farts when he eats and is already rather old. I'm so on edge and on top of it. The Rodrigues family tries to tell me that I don't care enough. They want to go to the hospital during the operation — what nerve! I convinced them to come here instead. Irene could not understand that I had not talked to the doctor. What's there to talk about? Those people are busy. I see no use in bothering them. My stomach feels closed and I eat only to keep my mother company.

June 11 — My birthday. 37 years. My mother put a cute card on the headrest, but how could I possibly feel cheerful with Ray going under the knife.

Then at 10 am they all came. Sally, Curly, Irene. We tried forcefully to make conversation. 11:45 the telephone rings. The doctor!? No. Ray. All is well and the operation over. It was so wonderful and hard to believe that I gulped down a cognac and offered drinks to everybody. Still there was fear in me. 2:30 We went to visit, and Ray was cheerful. At 7:30, he still was in good spirits. He even joked with my mother and was quite relaxed.

June 12 — He was already up when I got to the hospital. Although he walked with an effort, it was just marvelous to see. However, we are still waiting for the diagnosis of Dr. Yankifort. After all the horror stories of rectum ailments one is exposed to in the hospital, one cannot help imagining things. One man had hemorrhoids like oranges, and it turned out to be cancer. He was just 35 years old and just by a hair could be saved. I'm still nervous and on edge.

June 13 — Cooking three times a day to give my mother a good time. I'm just not up to taking her in to Manhattan or even to a restaurant. I buy her cherries and blueberries and little goodies to show that I care.

The doctor said Ray may come home tomorrow. How foolish to have worried so much, but rather to be

wrong that way. Bought a few colorful flowers to cheer up the garden. The roses are shortly to open.

June 14 — Ray is home again. I watch that he takes it easy. It is so hard for him to sit still. Two baths a day and early to bed.

I'm depressed because I heard about so many people quite young — Stanley 22, Jess 15 and even people I didn't know — just dying out of the blue. I'm scared to get a disease or Raymond getting one. But this is something one has to put out of one's mind.

June 15 — A pleasant day. Ray feels pretty good. We played dominoes with my mother at night. My mother is also a gambler. Marilyn is full of hate for husband. Barbara and Ed Reilly are in the seventh heaven....already talking about marriage.

June 16 — Brought my mother to the airport and got her a First Class seat after having been told that she would not get on the plane at all. Flight was crowded. I can't imagine what we'll be up to in July. My mother was very sweet and cried just a little. It all worked out very well. There is always the feeling that this time could be the last time. Who could predict the future?

June 18 — Had a spat with Ray. Probably because I am still quite moody and depressed.

A beautiful day crisp air and blue sky.

Met our neighbors in the $54,000 home. He is a big wheel with overseas airlines and very pleasant. She, Claire, has to be taken with a grain of salt I'm afraid. It was fun to go in the life raft and say hello to the people at the end of the canal whom one otherwise hardly ever meets.

I love to look at my flowers but it takes a lot of time to keep everything neat.

July 4 — Since it took five hours to fix the plane we went into town to buy antiques. A woman came into the place. A flaming redhead. She claimed she is a dealer, but she only picked the shop owners' brains asking questions about periods and makes. She was looking for a really good discount and the shop owner was annoyed because she was obviously just putting it on. We bought $120 worth of stuff and managed to get a 15% discount. Got two cabinets that are hard to find because they usually only have one piece left in good shape. He had plenty of carnival glass and even a few Tiffany pieces. Plates are real expensive because they are old pieces left from collections, but I have seen them ridiculously priced in antique shows in the States.

Waiting for our plane at PIK. It's delayed out of New York and now it has to circle because of an SAS DC-8 coming in with hydraulic emergency. A charter plane with 104 passengers crashed in the Pyrenees near Barcelona. There might be a maintenance delay on our plane also. The Captain has lost his suitcase at JFK and is in a bad mood. I woke up with an earache. I would like to go to Schwabing but probably have no energy left. I mailed a letter to my mother through Pan American traffic in Stuttgart. Curious to see if they will send it because originally they wanted money for it.

July 6 — PIK/JFK A full flight and again it was one of the sub loads who got drunk and was most demanding. Came in through some light thunderstorms and I kept thinking about the two airplane crashes — one in Spain and one in Toronto during the last two days. Both jets and a total of 201 people killed.

July 12 — Prague early in the morning. A restless night on hard beds, while people next door had a party and one could hear the highly intelligent doodah, etc. Lots of people from tour groups up and around already. The waitress is German. A Kraut knows a Kraut. She speaks German with me. It is an hour till pickup. I still have to go upstairs again and change. But it is so much more relaxing to have breakfast without the uniform. Let's see if I can get another cup of coffee. I asked her very nicely and she is sweet. She looks like one of the Kranzler girls. If you know Berlin Germany, you know Kranzler is a coffee house on the Kurfürstendamm.

July 30 — Captain Gray had his 19-year-old daughter and his wife Anne on the flight to SNN, and we made a little small talk after dinner in the dining room. They're going to Berlin with us tomorrow. Anne is a real Southerner, a bleached blonde with a slurring voice and the obvious desire to be pleasant and liked. They live in Bermuda, and we will probably exchange addresses.

August 4 — Mark, my nephew, missed his plane in Paris. He was in the toilet when they called the standbys so he had to stay an extra day without money in Paris. He didn't get any pocket money during the entire trip and couldn't even get postage to write us a postcard. That does not sound true, but maybe I have the wrong idea about an 18-year-old boy.

August 5 — Captain Charles Morris JFK/CPH. He brought me some pillows into the cockpit and invited me to rest, which I thought extremely nice and it relaxed me quite a bit. There was very little to do with 33 passengers total. Had a very nice couple in First Class. They travel three months out of the year and were very appreciative of our First Class service. It was a pleasure to serve them. In seat 4A was an old bald guy secretly on the war path. Groups of unattractive beings in the back. I know that's mean, but those people look as if they all won prizes for oddities at a TV contest. They smell too. I have to hold my breath while I'm going down the elevator with an elderly couple. Their faces are blank but they are loaded with educational sightseeing equipment. The cafeteria is alright if one likes spaghetti and warm beer.

August 7 — A shuttle to Stockholm. Bought some Swedish books. I can read and understand every single word, but am unable any longer to speak the language. It's like a mental block. I am missing the simplest expressions.

August 8 — CPH/JFK This hotel is a 20-minute bus ride away from the city. Sleep is good but today we are just staying in bed out of boredom and that seems a shame. A bright sun is shining into the room. Children are playing in the street. The maid came in. She must be surprised that we never got up. But the minute I do get up I am aware of some pains and this makes me want to go right back into bed. This is no real challenge. It's a period of lethargy and Ray has joined in.

August 9 — It was a full flight back. Getting home Sally and Curly thought they'd entertain us. Any flight for them is fun. They do not get it that it can be work.

August 14 — JFK/CPH Sat on a hot sticky airplane full of passengers for 1.5 hours and we all got sick. A stupid way to run an airline. Had weird passengers. One First Class lady passenger was missing a bag and insisted she had handed it to us. I got the bright idea that it might have been changed in the Clipper Lounge and so it was. Passenger in 2C complained that the food is poor and why didn't we serve caviar. Passenger in 1A got sick because her suitcase could not be found.

August 15 — Copenhagen again. Got myself gooseberries — the first in a long time. Then we slept and had a picnic at night. Then slept again. Sure there are things to do. One could take the hydrofoil to Malmo, go to the Tivoli or just walk around. But all that is not really important and holds very little interest to me when I am tired.

We are already changing crew hotels again next week. From then on it's the SAS hotel at the airport.

August 16 — CPH Flight 95 to Arlington. Had a deportee. A heavy prisoner accompanied by a policeman who could take James Bond's place. Benson, a US citizen, had tried for the third time to get into Sweden where as a tale goes he has been thrown out originally because of molesting girls.

Furthermore, just before departure a message came for a Mrs. Johnson saying she did not get on the flight. She was a passenger on a prepaid ticket. However, we didn't open the doors again but took off to the States.

September 8 — It's the 8th September here because we flew over the dateline. Tokyo for the first time in 12 years of flying. Staying at the hotel the new Otani. The thought "where do they bury their people?" occurred to me on the drive from the airport,

December — Sorry I could not continue my diary because flights became too bumpy, too crowded, too back-to-back and less interesting. ✈

Certificates

Pan American World Airways had a way of making its employees feel appreciated. Achievement medals and certificates were distributed to those who earned them.

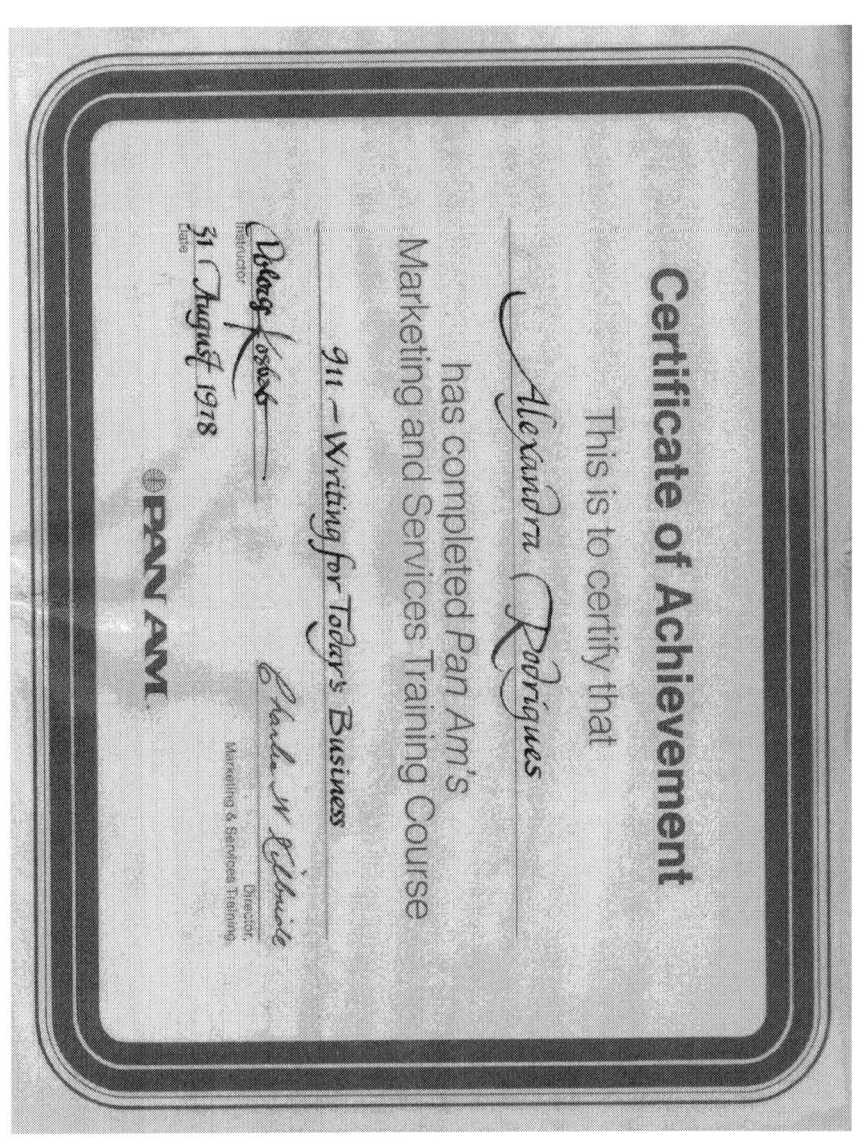

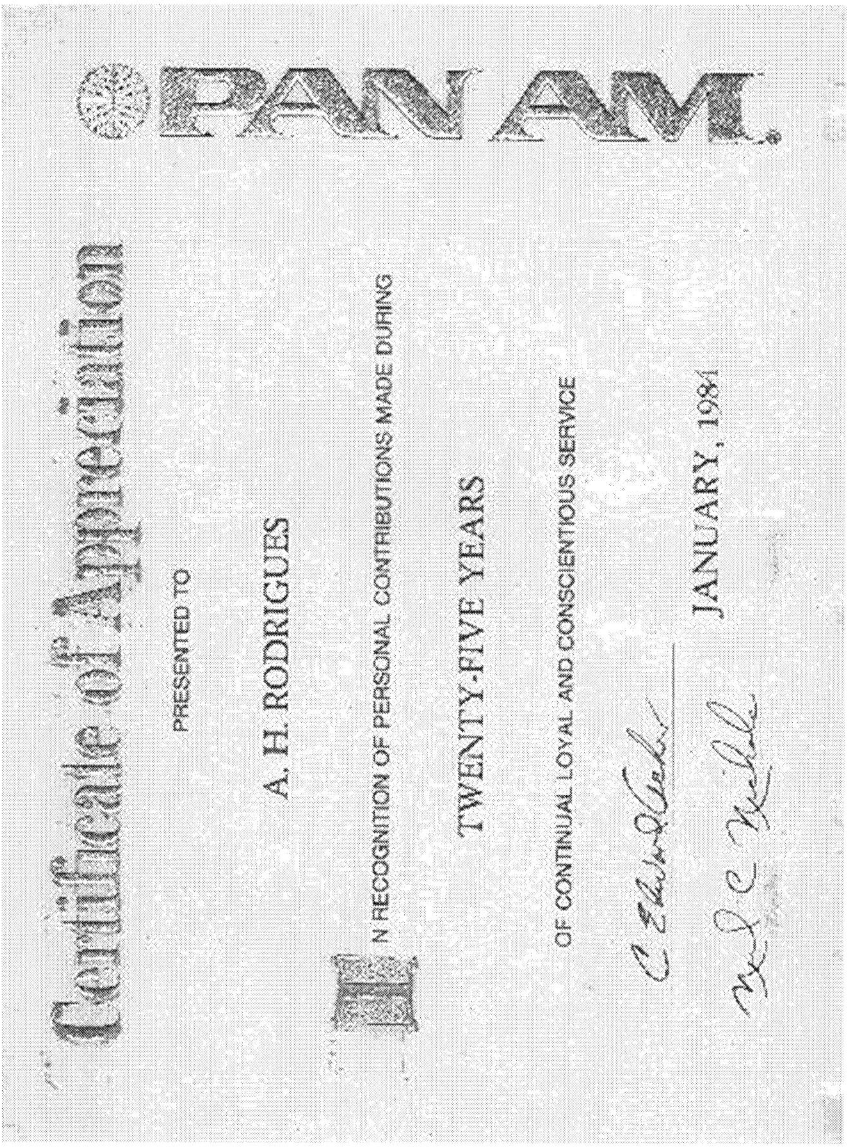

PAN AM.

Certificate of Appreciation

PRESENTED TO

A. H. RODRIGUES

IN RECOGNITION OF PERSONAL CONTRIBUTIONS MADE DURING

TWENTY-FIVE YEARS

OF CONTINUAL LOYAL AND CONSCIENTIOUS SERVICE

JANUARY, 1984

This is to certify that

Raymond Rodriguez

was selected to participate in
the inauguration of Pan American's
Jet Clipper service
between
U.S.A. and Europe

Sept. 7, 1958
DATE

H. R. GRAY

PAN AM

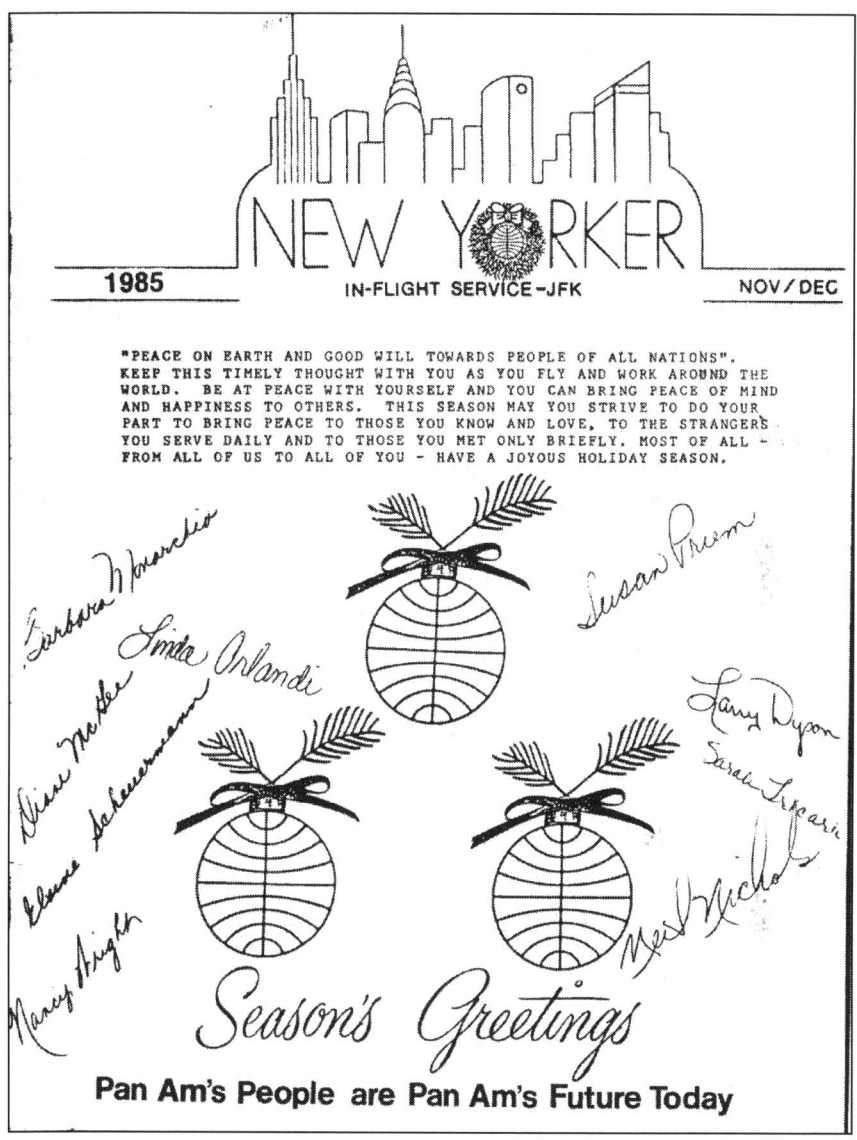

Print communication was more important in a world before the internet.

Management

It was 1971. It had been confirmed that I was pregnant with a due date of April 1972. Everything in my life had changed lately and was to change even more in the future as I now know. I was one of the first stewardesses who would be allowed to return to flight status after having given birth. In the meantime, I was offered a temporary position in flight service management, which I accepted gratefully.

I became a Girl Friday with the title of Supervisor. Whenever a supervisor was ill, quit or for whatever reason could not perform their job, I had to fill in. This way, I soon had my hands in everything:

- The briefing office, with a very unhealthy schedule and many night shifts. It was the office where crews reported for emergency briefing, grooming check and last-minute passenger advisories.
- The medical desk, where flight attendants would call in sick and I had to coordinate with flight dispatch to find replacement for the sick person's next trip.
- The charter desk, where we assigned charter positions to flight attendants according to language qualification, nationality and seniority. I also was responsible for getting valid visas for the flight attendants on those charters.
- The accounting desk, a position that nobody wanted, became my main responsibility. I had to ensure that expense reports were looked at and, within reason, payments were made to flight attendants. This included meal expenses, laundry bills and other payments incurred during layovers. When flight attendants were furloughed

or quit, I had to collect from them any outstanding monies owed to the company.

✈ The flight service department had to prepare an annual budget to be sent to headquarters by a given deadline. As I had been trained in this function by the supervisor Sandy Peters who had this desk before me, I ended up doing all the work meant for the manager. I did the budget! I got a thank you from the manager but headquarters would never find out; it was not mentioned in my evaluation. Each supervisor and manager was subject to an evaluation once a year. After Pan American had gone Chapter 11, I often joked, "I did the budgets for Pan Am. No wonder they went bankrupt." Of course, there was no truth to it.

My son Raymond grew up handsomely.

Two months before my due date, I took a leave of absence and was to return to flight status six weeks after giving birth. Easier said than done. Although we had live-in help from day one, my husband and I decided that one of us should be reachable at all times. We knew that our time flying together was over. Even getting a schedule where our flights would not overlap was nearly impossible. For a while, there were schedules that let my husband fly turn-arounds: For example, leave early in the morning for Santa Domingo and return that same evening to New York City.

All this did not work out for us, so I returned to management. I had worked for small companies in Germany as secretary, but I was not used to in-house competition and the infighting that exists within a company as large as Pan American. Any effort to be promoted failed. While in management I was finally offered a position with Dr. Bator, the director of language development.

Alexandra on left and Dr. Bator at right.

The work with the language lab was easy and enjoyable. I worked on vocabulary lists: French, Spanish and German. I assisted flight attendants when they came in to listen to tapes.

Pan American Flight Service management consisted of three main sections:

- ✈ Personnel Supervisors
- ✈ Briefing Office
- ✈ Administration

Personnel Supervisors

Personnel Supervisors were responsible for attitude, grooming and in-flight passenger relations. My only experience here was being part of the hiring committee during one season.

Most of my time in Flight Service management was spent in Administration. I handled every single desk at one time or another. Most of my connections have been lost during the decades since the airline folded its wings in 1991. Here are the names of some of my coworkers I was able to locate.

Ann Claps

Ann Claps was in charge of the Charter Desk. Ann had started to work for Pan Am in 1948. She was one the first supervisors I was assigned to.

The new Snow Ball Queen and her court pose for Royal Photographer MICHAEL STANLEY. Left to right the dazzling damsels are: ANN CLAPS, EVELYN WIEDMANN, 1947's Snow Ball Queen JEAN FOLEY, 1951's Queen DOROTHY BURKE, HELEN DREGAN and TERRY DE SALVIO. In the background are SEYMOUR BERMAN, ED CORRIGAN, and Vice President HAROLD R. HARRIS.

Ann and her husband became dear family friends. Jerry Claps worked for the Pan Am Federal Credit Union after he had retired from the Police Department. He and my son loved each other dearly. Jerry passed away in 2005 and Ann passed at the age of 96 in 2015.

Susan Boyle

Susan Boyle nee Gregory was in charge of Administration. She married a Police Officer. After the end of Pan Am they moved from city to city. Every Christmas I have to change the address in my phone book. Sue has become an artist and lives in Denton, Texas. I have kept in touch with her all along.

Clare Christensen

Clare Christensen was one of my bosses in management. She is very involved in Pan Am Ex-Employee activities. A widow by now for many years.

Dick Tinsler

Dick Tinsler was a personnel supervisor. I am in contact with him on FaceBook.

Diane Matthews

Diane Matthews was kind enough to contribute some of her memories:

I was "promoted" from the Manhattan F/S office F/S status in early 1972 to be Supervisor and sort of all-round bottle-washer at Houston with Alex Bridgers (now deceased) for a new F/S base that the Company was opening up there. So, I was in Houston from 1972-74 almost exactly to the day.

Ann Claps seated at left.

In early 1974, there was the oil crisis and other stuff going on globally, so I elected to transfer back to New York City. At that time, (I hope my memory is correct) I was a Personnel Supervisor, Flight Supervisor and also was a Supervisor in the Briefing Office...all that from about 1974-'78.

I remember almost daily coming from the back of the Hangar where our Personnel Supervisory offices were located to the front area to speak with either Joe or John. Joe Vissicchio, then later John Iannone were the Base Managers and Hope Walden had a job up there too, along with Edna Myers. I don't remember what Hope's title was.

I do remember one incident of a stewardess whom I supervised, being put out because she had to come out to the Hangar from her apartment in Manhattan for an office chat with me. From the report received from the Purser on her flight, it seems she had simply walked off her airplane at some transit point in the Caribbean and got on another Pan Am flight going back to New York (sitting on a jump seat) because she wanted to see her boyfriend back in the City! When I talked to her, I distinctly remember my mind being so boggled because she could not understand why on earth she was being reprimanded!

Another time, there had been a huge write-up in the latest edition of *New York Magazine* about the new mysterious disease cropping up called toxoplasmosis—due, apparently, from so much litter from dogs on all the streets of Manhattan. Or was it pigeon droppings? – both? All of us in the office were talking about this new "disease thing" and was it credible or not.

The next thing I knew, another stewardess of "mine" complained all the way to either Joe or John about a medical letter I had previously sent her outlining all the numerous absences this particular girl had taken over the past 8-9 months of flying. Her excuse, among other reasons for her extreme absenteeism, was that she had now contacted this new illness - toxoplasmosis. There was no doctor's report in the file I saw. As I recall, it was a self-diagnosis.

On the lighter side, I remember going out to lunch occasionally with Susan Priem in her car to the nearest place we could find a pizza or something quick, cheap and Italian. It always turned out to be in some Howard Beach place where we used to giggle, laugh and were convinced we were eating next to Mafioso. Maybe we were? All those guys in black suits and cigs facing the door?

Ray Calouri

Ray Calouri from Crew Scheduling. A department working closely with Flight Scheduling. I would have liked to work there  but was only asked to substitute when they had extreme shortage of people. I remember the tracking of the flights on the blackboards which Flight Scheduling from JFK was assigned and that position reminded me of the importance of the air traffic controllers.

Briefing Office

The briefing office required shift work. During many night shifts, I helped prepare paperwork for the Flight Service crews that would report for morning departures. Punctuality was the most important issue. A flight does not wait. Neatness and grooming were also strictly observed.

I worked the Medical Desk, did budgets, organized Visas for entries of F/S into various foreign countries, handled passenger complaints and on and on. ✈

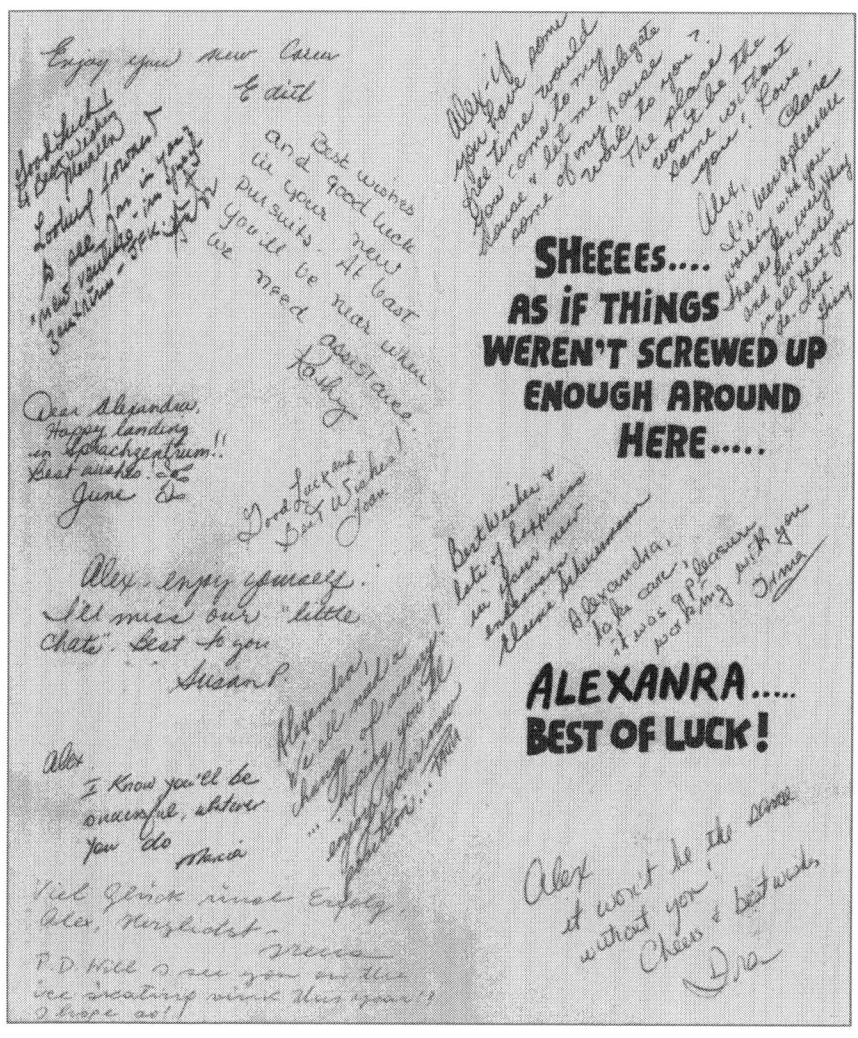

Ready to Begin flying out of the New York base. Accompanied by good wishes of the management group responsible for our initial training. It had to be 1959. I only recognize a few names. Maybe you will recognize the signature of one of your parents or grandparents.

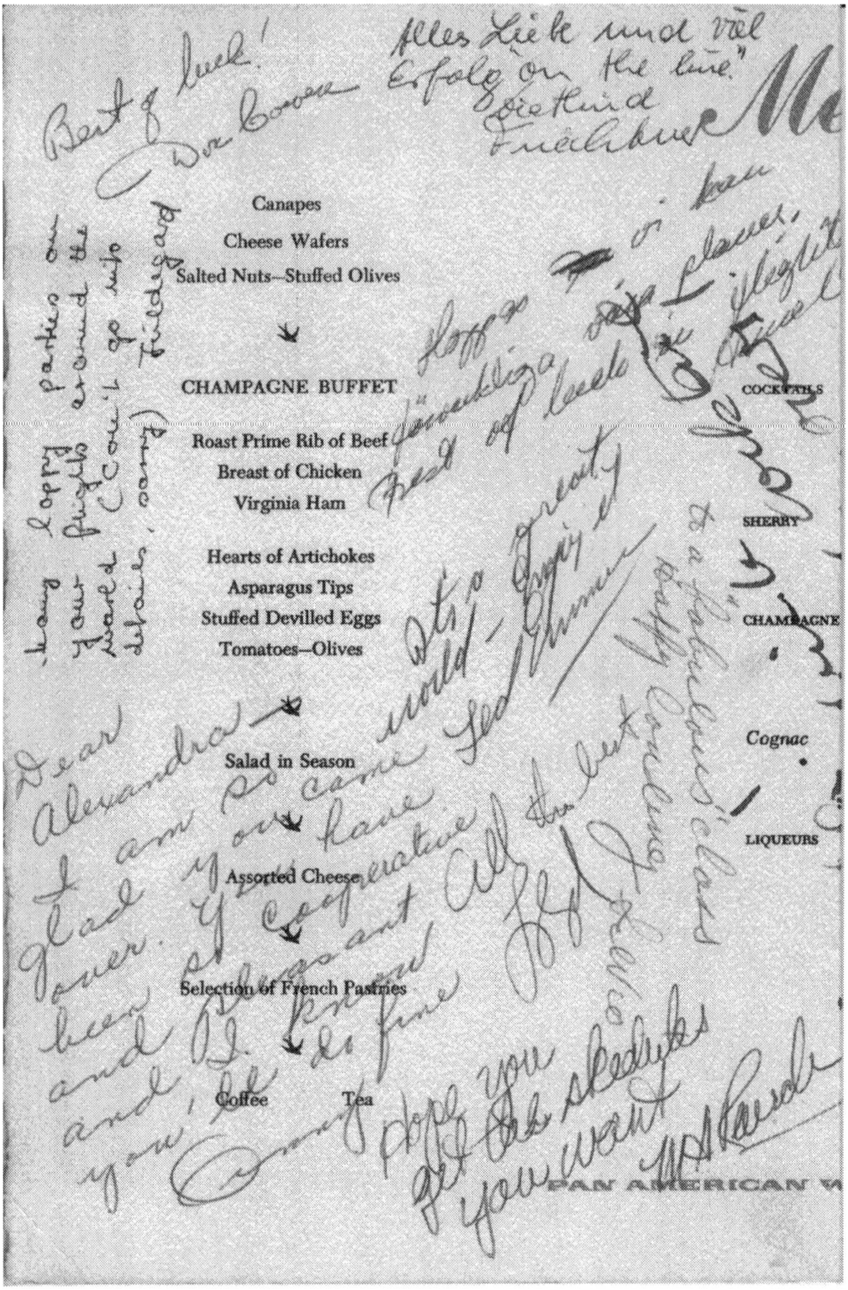

Canapes

Cheese Wafers

Salted Nuts–Stuffed Olives

CHAMPAGNE BUFFET

Roast Prime Rib of Beef

Breast of Chicken

Virginia Ham

Hearts of Artichokes

Asparagus Tips

Stuffed Devilled Eggs

Tomatoes–Olives

Salad in Season

Assorted Cheese

Selection of French Pastries

Coffee Tea

COCKTAILS

SHERRY

CHAMPAGNE

Cognac

LIQUEURS

PAN AMERICAN W

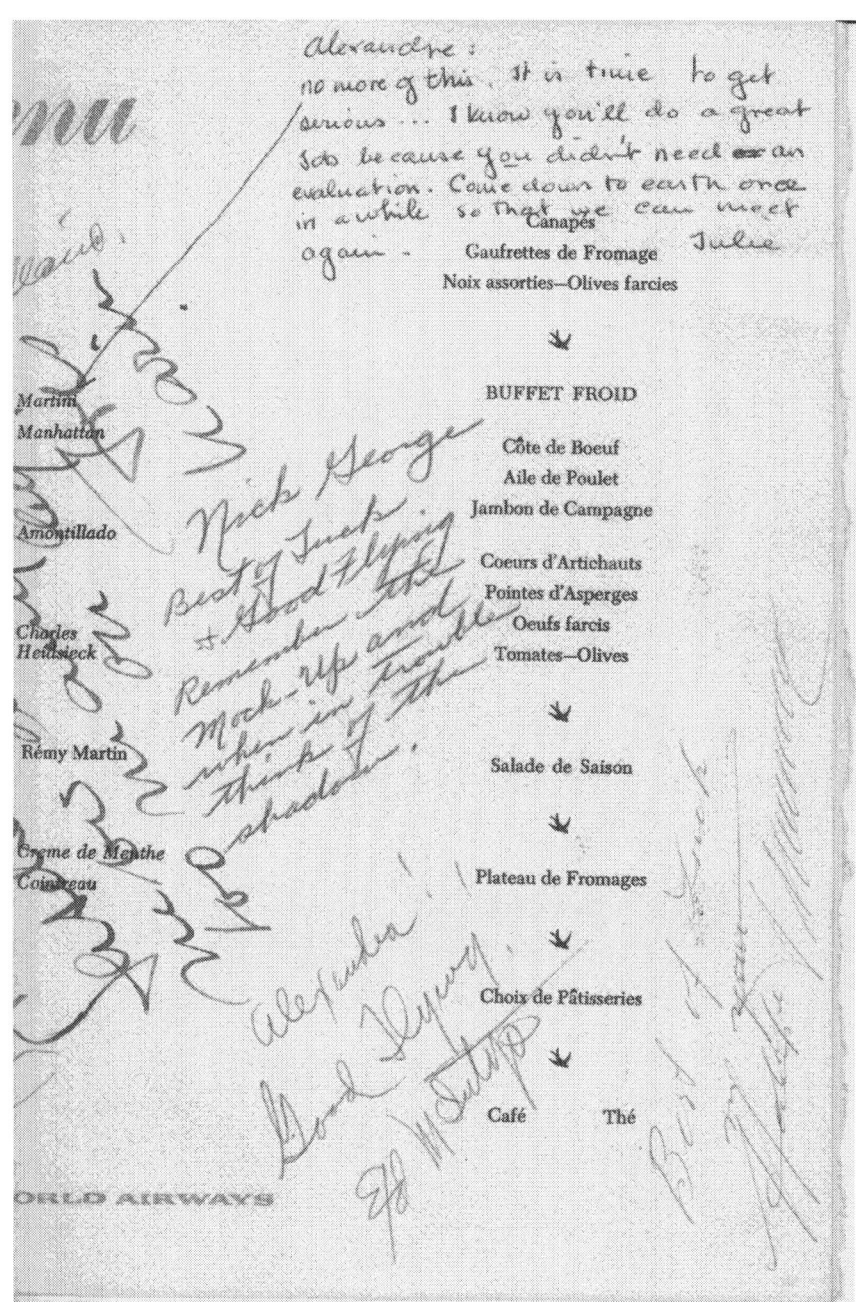

Alexandre:
no more of this. It is time to get serious... I know you'll do a great job because you didn't need an evaluation. Come down to earth once in a while so that we can meet again.
— Julie

Martini
Manhattan

Amontillado

Charles
Heidsieck

Rémy Martin

Crème de Menthe
Cointreau

Nick George
Best of luck
+ Good Flying.
Remember the
Mock-Up and
when in trouble
think of the
shadow.

Alexander!
Good flying!
EH McDuffee

Canapés
Gaufrettes de Fromage
Noix assorties—Olives farcies

☟

BUFFET FROID

Côte de Boeuf
Aile de Poulet
Jambon de Campagne

Coeurs d'Artichauts
Pointes d'Asperges
Oeufs farcis
Tomates—Olives

☟

Salade de Saison

☟

Plateau de Fromages

☟

Choix de Pâtisseries

☟

Café   Thé

Fairbanks, Alaska

It is a truly cold morning, here on February 13, 2016 in New York City. They are expecting record-setting cold temperatures by tomorrow. Minus 2° F last occurred in 1916. They are predicting the wind-chill factor will make it feel like minus 20° F.

Inside my house, the bright sun mocks this news as it warms the carpet where its rays are concentrating. Stay inside, the radio warns. Why not? This does give me the leisure to reminisce.

It must have been about 1962. We landed with a 707 Boeing, one of the first jets, in Fairbanks, Alaska. It was February. In Alaska, which is the gateway to the Arctic Circle, the temperatures from October through March vary from minus 2° up to 14° F.

A ground crew dressed in Eskimo attire had come to meet the plane. They labored to put up the old-fashioned metallic stairway with its platform on top where it reached the cabin door. We, the crew, had to wait for their knock at the front door before removing the emergency shoot attachment and opening up. Only one door was to be opened no matter how many passengers on board. This was to minimize the amount of freezing air rushing into the cabin of the plane. Immediately after the door was opened, crew and passengers were supplied with heavy parkas, woolly face covers with ear muffs and furry gloves.

Electrically powered cars were attached with immense wires to loading stations that looked like parking meters. In them we were taken to a motel near the airport.

I recall it was only a few steps from the room, across the parking lot, over to the cafeteria. Nevertheless, one had to bundle up, in order to prevent frostbite. These are experiences I will never forget. They make today's temperature here in New York feel like a day in spring. It is at least six months the norm in Alaska, while we are looking at two days the most here in New York and vicinity

There is plenty of beauty in Alaska too. At some times during the year, mostly in June, July and August it can be pleasantly warm. There had been trips to Fairbanks, when I would take walks at a nearby lake and wore nothing but a short-sleeved dress. Alaska is also known for a Midnight Sun Festival in June, when the sun never sets. This spectacular I unfortunately missed but can picture it vividly in my mind.

Nowadays cruises to Alaska are in fashion. I am sure they are an exciting and delightful experience. ✈

Paris Memoir

Memoir comes from the French word Memoires and the Latin based word Memoria. So it seems a given to focus on Paris, the city of the Louvre with the Venus de Milo, the Arc de Triumph and Sacre Coeur de Montmartre.

What once was the description of a recent trip to Paris, namely in the year 1968, is now, 46 years later a memoir. Paris has charm, its language is melodious and its heart is the people.

We stayed at the Hotel Terrace in the suburb Neuilly, 20 minutes by tram from the Champs Elysees, the Broadway of Paris. The elegant lobby furnished in Louis XIV (1638-1715) style featured armchairs with exquisite Petit Point covers. Large mirrors in heavy frames and crystal chandeliers contributed to the luxury. A cozy wood-burning fireplace near the bar, where authentic Cognac from the province Cognac was served in shallow goblets, and a dining room with velvet wallpaper, evoked thoughts of the Renaissance.

About 7 pm my husband and I walked through the dimly lit, narrow streets to a restaurant, usually ten minutes away. It took us half an hour to get there. In Italy you would call it a Trattoria. Students, Priests and artists favored that place. My husband used to say, "Eat where the Priests eat if you want good food." Right he was. The Hors d'oeuvre is plentiful. One need's to wash them down with some French wine or Perrier water to make room for the entrée. On the narrow street, a truck and a yellow Peugeot were nearly locked, windshield to windshield, neither one of them willing to yield. They tooted their horns and other cars, unable to pass, joined into the concert. A group of passers-by cheered them on, laughing and cursing at the same time.

Despite the delay we were the first guests. Supper in France does not start till after the Theatre and Opera. In our broken French we ordered and savored a bottle of Bordeaux 1961 while the freshly baked French bread stimulated our taste buds. The menu was handwritten and we guessed more than really knowing what we were ordering. All French food is good; we could hardly go wrong. Most chefs had trained at Maxim's International, the famous French restaurant, known to every gourmet. French conversation began to echo around us, as the little tables with the checkered red and white tablecloths began to fill. Mellow classic music came out of recessed loudspeakers, tantalizing the senses. A flower girl offered roses and violets. My husband bought me violets with raindrops hanging on their velvety leaves. I pinned them smilingly on the collar of my trench coat. By that time candles had been lit on every table, stressing the romantic atmosphere. To top off our splurge in delicacies, my husband and I shared a Lavender Crème brûlée, a popular French dessert. Arm in arm we went back under a light mist and breathed in the romance of Paris

This was a trip about 1970. Paris was always dear to me. My first trip, away from what was then my hometown, was in

1958. During WW II my father found refuge in Paris to avoid the Nazi camps. When flying as stewardess, I bid for Paris trips frequently and came to know the city and its beautiful surroundings quite well. So you see, a part of my heart belongs to Paris. It is wounded now. It will heal. It is a city of beauty, of culture, of architectural treasures and above all, of strength. Vive La France, the city with everlasting charm. ✈

From the Wine Cellars of Pan Am, we have selected a variety of fine wines to complement your in-flight meal service

Your Flight Attendant can advise you of today's available selection

U. S. Domestic Flights

Domaine Chandon Blanc de Noirs
Buena Vista Zinfandel 1982   Buena Vista Chardonnay 1983

International Flights

Dom Perignon
Moët et Chandon Brut Imperial Rose Vintage
Moët et Chandon Brut Imperial
Moreau et Fils Mâcon Villages 1983
Georges Duboeuf Bourgogne Aligoté 1982
Georges Duboeuf Mâcon Villages 1984
Georges Duboeuf Fleurie 1982
Robert Mondavi Cabernet Sauvignon 1980
Georges Duboeuf Julienas 1982   Monterrey Zinfandel 1984
Rutherford Hill Cabernet Sauvignon 1981
Rutherford Hill Chardonnay 1983

Regional Wines

in markets serving their country of origin

France - Les Fortes de Latour Pauillac 1977
Germany - Geisenheimer Rothenberg Riesling 1982   Argentina - San Telmo Chardonnay 1984
Switzerland - Cure d'Attalens Lavaux 1982   Switzerland - Dôle Sang de Lenfer 1983
Italy - Antinori Chianti Classico Reserve 1980

Thinking of Food

Going through my Pan Am memorabilia, I came across several menus from our Lunch and Dinner Services in First Class. It was then that I realized how blasé I had become through the years. From nearly starving through the War years and being thrilled with dandelion salad and greasy, grimy leftovers from Russian soldiers' canteen food (when a slice of toasted cornbread with fatty bacon was a delicacy exclusively for holidays), I have risen to become part of the top of culinary consumers.

Orange blossoms (Champagne and freshly squeezed orange juice) for breakfast or a Bloody Mary (vodka and tomato juice spiced with horseradish and decorated with a slice of fresh lemon) after a night of walking up and down the aisles of a transatlantic jet serving passengers was commonplace when arriving at a crew hotel for a 24-hour layover.

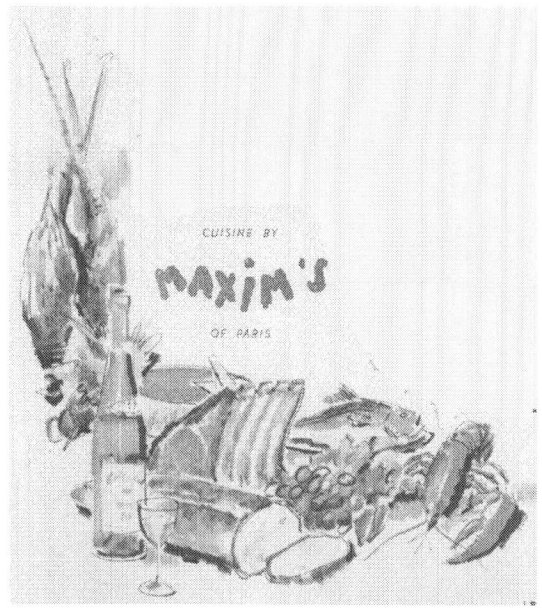

Lunch was often taken at airport restaurants anywhere from New York to Zurich to Rome, Beirut, Tehran, Karachi, Hong Kong, Dakar, Johannesburg to Dar es Salaam, Tanzania (where the blue Tanzanite gem comes from). The tanzanite has become quite a gemstone of choice demanding a high price now. I could have picked it up cheap, but I did not do so. Another opportunity missed.

Memories of bratwurst in Germany, curry dishes in New Delhi, and Calderada, a soup made with at least six different kinds of fish, in Portugal still today make my taste buds tingle. While we were indulging on those local tidbits, the aircraft was provisioned by the station's commissary with superb specialties of the respective country and the ever-standard juicy prime rib of beef which we cooked and served rare, medium or well done to those passengers unwilling to indulge in unfamiliar fare.

Menu cover celebrating the anniversary of the Statue of Liberty

A Dinner menu consisted of cocktails, hors d'oeuvres, fish, a main entrée of choice, cheeses from all over the world and dessert of irresistible quality, like Cherries Jubilee or vanilla ice cream with a thick chocolate sauce. All this was followed by cordials.

French wine, Brut Champagne and beer were available without limitations – in First Class that is! I became an expert in popping Champagne corks and am still admired for my dexterity in it. Here are a few dishes I will never forget. Russian caviar, served with chopped egg and lemon slices, accompanied by Stolichnaya Vodka. Lobster Thermidor. Quail with grapes. Cornish Hen. Veal chops with Calvados sauce. Pâté foie gras and truffles. Not to forget the Cherries Jubilee: Sour cherries slightly heated, and, served over heart-melting vanilla ice cream. Well, I am getting carried away and hungry. A good espresso for digestion to end the feast in style.

On international layovers of several days in the 1960s and 1970s, I made it a habit to sample the native delicacies: Kippers for breakfast in Scotland, avocado and eel in Mexico, chorizo and eggs in Portugal, venison with lingonberries in Sweden, sushi in Japan. Different roasts from the carving board in England, Kobe beef in Guam, turtle soup, goulash and a multitude more. Today I would settle for oysters and Eggs Benedict. I guess you can understand that my taste has been spoiled, confused and quite unconventional during the years.

I am thinking about world-renowned chefs! My husband could have joined their ranks. He loved to cook. He had worked as a butler for several mega-rich families where the old ladies loved him as he was very handsome.

Only the best chefs worked for those families. My husband had plenty of opportunity to mingle and taste the Pheasant Under Glass, the Beef Wellington and more. From there Pan Am got hold of him, and they sent him to become acquainted with the services of superb dining at Maxim's in Paris. He was not to learn to cook, but to excel in the elegant ways of serving food. All through my marriage I profited from those experiences. ✈

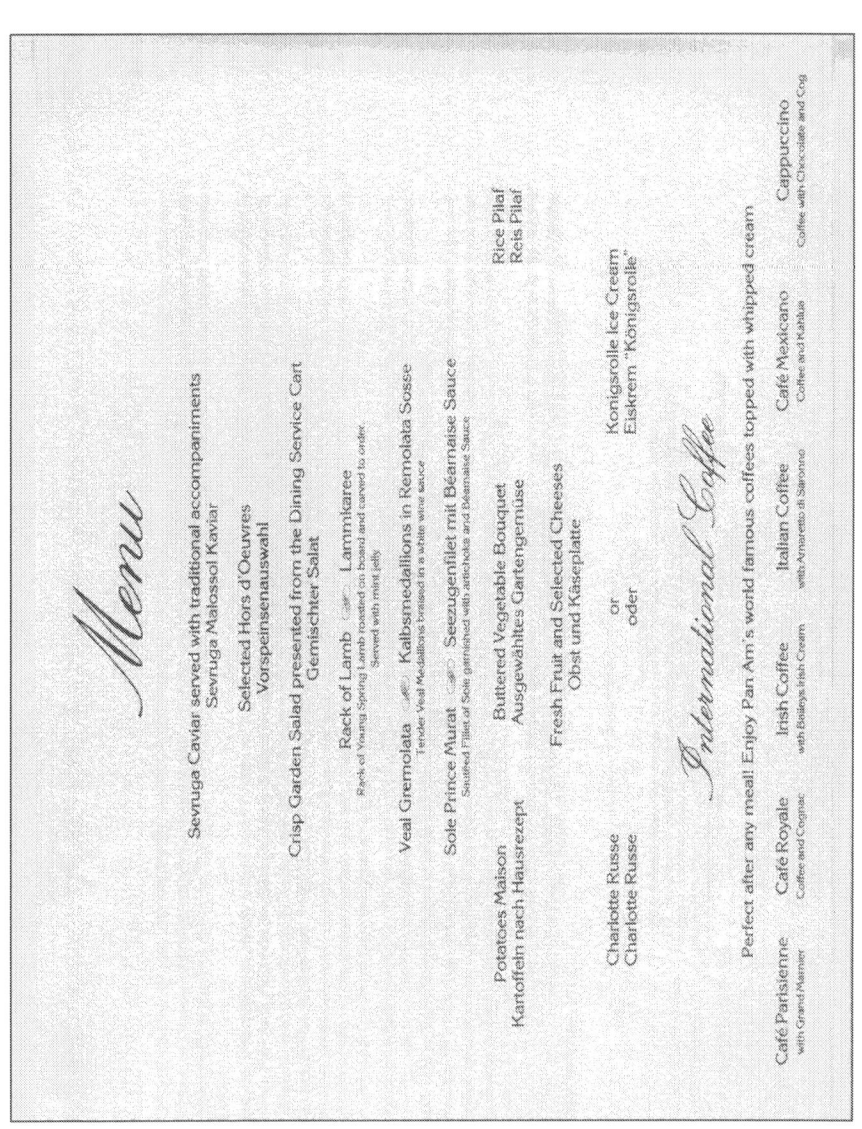

Turkey, Turkey

What about Turkey? Are we talking about Turkey, the country in the Middle East? Its capital is Istanbul, in old times called Constantinople. Istanbul's main attractions are its Mosques and of course for me its bazaars. A stroll along the tent-like boutiques could keep me entertained for hours. The vendors would invite me in to their cubicles when they sensed that I was interested in some of their wares. I would be asked to sit on a three-legged stool and be served a demitasse of espresso that nearly stood up in the little cup. How could I not buy anything after such cordial treatment?

I floated along the Bosporus toward the Black Sea on a boat crowded with tourists. At the stately Hilton Hotel, where I stayed, I would take a shower and then go to the inviting swimming pool. As skin cancer was hardly ever talked about at that time, bikini beauties were soaking up the sun in comfortable deck chairs, many of them with a Piña Colada in hand. I joined them.

Turkey? The plan was to talk about turkey, the bird. I do have an excuse for having gotten side-tracked. I was already in my twenties when I heard about turkey, the bird, for the first time. In Germany, we did not have turkeys nor did we have Thanksgiving. After the harvest we had a thankful celebration called Erntedankfest but turkey was not part of it. My first Thanksgiving in the States introduced me to the poultry turkey. As a Flight Attendant I had to serve it to passengers in First Class, carving in from a board on a serving cart, in front of the guests. Luckily we had had extensive galley training before flaunting our culinary arts in flight. Why the name turkey for the bird. During global trade in old times a bird called Guinea fowl shipped from Africa. It became known as "Turkey cock" as it had come via Constantinople, an important hub of international trade, into England. Later British settlers brought it into the United States, and it was simply called turkey.

I remember a turkey fiasco that happened when I introduced my parents in Germany to their first turkey. My husband and I had bought a huge frozen turkey and managed to get it to Berlin, still frozen after resting it on the lid of the icebox on the plane, which held the ice cubes for the cocktail service. Our enthusiasm had gone overboard. My mother's oven was much too small. We had to let it defrost and the next day my husband cut it into pieces. We ate turkey for many days. It all defeated the purpose of having a crisp, enticing bird on a big platter, inviting us to a meal.

Ironically, the name of turkeys in the Turkish language, is Hindi, short for bird from India. It seems the Turks may have originally thought that those birds came from India – thanks to a little miscalculation by Columbus.

I will end here, not to confuse the issue any further and not to spoil all our appetite for the next Thanksgiving dinner. ✈

In-Flight Entertainment

Through the years, the in-flight entertainment became more and more manifold. A cocktail service was standard. In First Class, French Champagne and popular German and French wines were available at all times. Alcohol is said to be twice as potent at 30,000 feet as on the ground. It costs passengers to court in-flight attendants with poems, pictures, love letters and the like. Posted for eternity on dinner menus, cocktail napkins, or in-flight stationery. I spent many hours in the First Class lounge playing cards or chess with otherwise bored passengers. *The New York Times* crossword puzzle or the easier task of the *Herald Tribune* puzzle offered further entertainment. ✈

Artistic passengers passed time sketching on menu folders.

Many art styles were demonstrated.

I, Emory Moore, being of unsound mind and woefully inadequate in body — albeit of good cheer — do hereby give, devise and bequeath unto my friend (mon ami) Senor a Rodrigues all my right, title and interest in and to an undivided 11/27 interest in my holdings in Summitt Lumber Co, Inc, Los Angeles Calif.

Sometimes a little too much champagne could lead to sworn empty promises.

Playing cards and magazines were always available.

For the Younger Set

Pan American World Airways did provide diversions for children traveling the skies. Do you remember Pierre & Penny Panda?

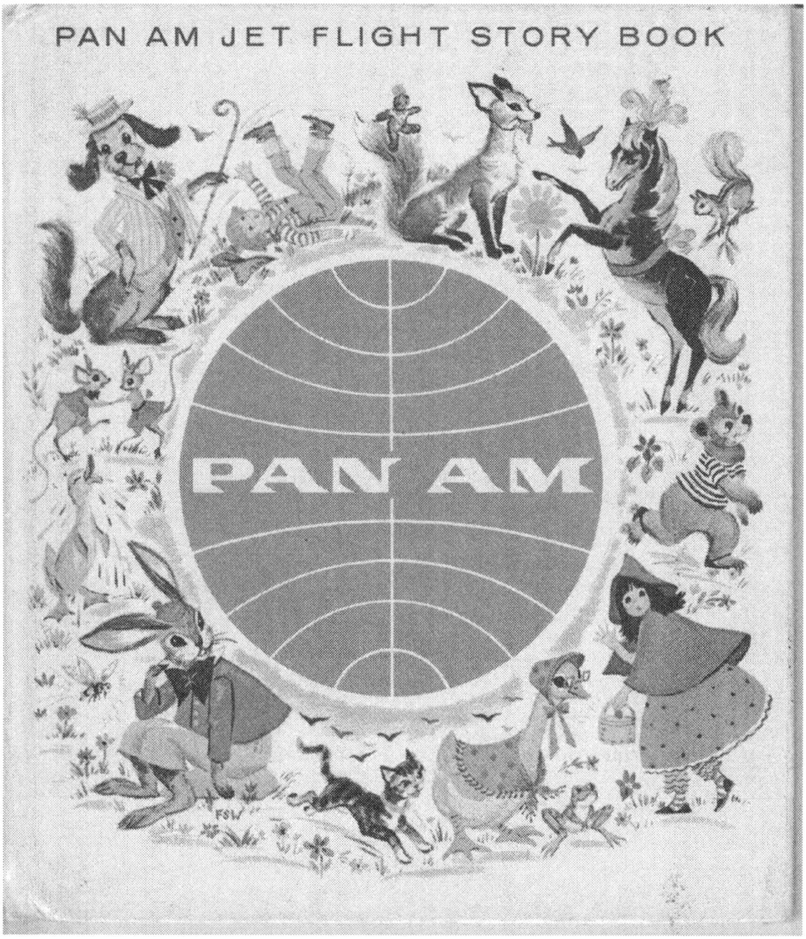
PAN AM JET FLIGHT STORY BOOK
PAN AM

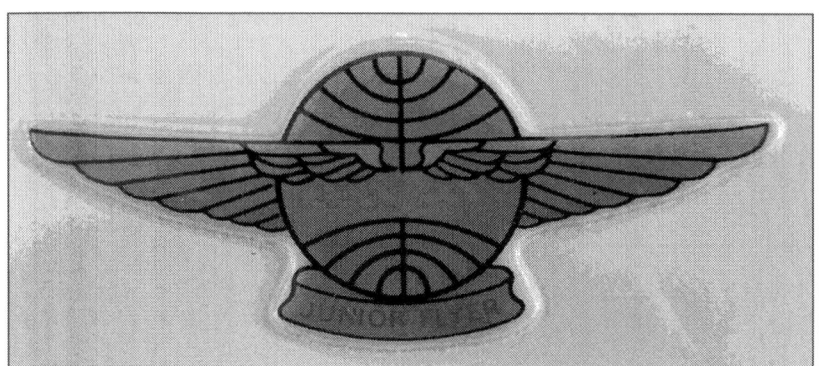

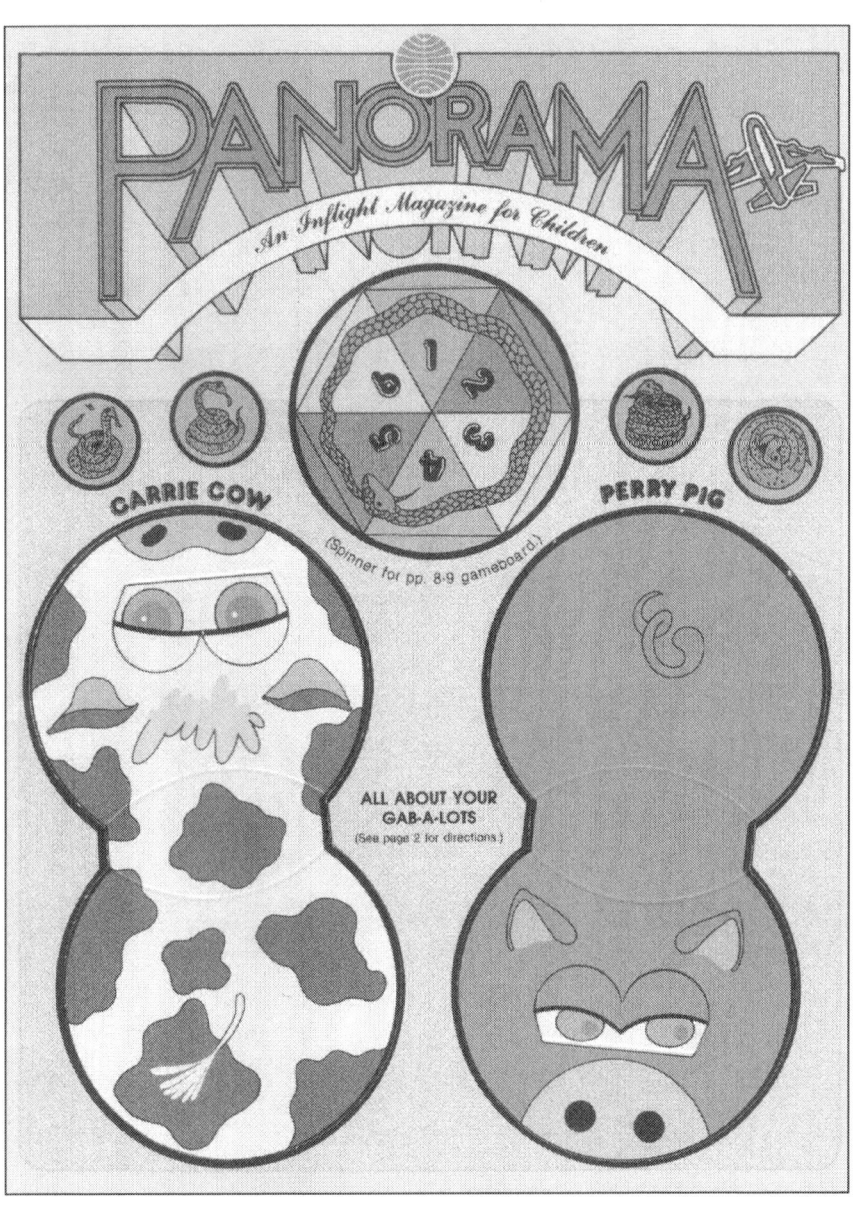

At the Airport

Planes, planes, planes – People, people, people.

Metallic, disembodied voices announce arrivals, departures or more often than not, delays over the loudspeaker of the International Terminal.

At the ramps, all types and sizes of aircraft rev up their engines before they swing up into the air and wing through the sound barrier.

People don't walk; they hustle. Some hurry toward the entrances, others rush toward the exits, from left to right, from front to back. They push and pull suitcases and cabin luggage ahead or behind.

If you take the time to watch closely, you will find myriad emotions hidden in the ongoing commotion. The airport is a stage for drama stored up until finally being released, right here, where thousands of people part and meet.

Near a check-in counter, kneeling on the stone floor, a small blond blue-eyed boy is happily playing with a toy plane. He's unconcerned that people might trip over him. His father is busy with filling out travel documents. Only now and then he shoots his son a stern glance. The cheeks of the little chap are flushed with excitement. Soon, for the first time, he will be in a real airplane. Together with his Daddy he will fly to see Grandma. What he doesn't know yet is that he will have to stay with Grandma for a long time. His parents have gotten divorced. His mother is in prison and his father does not have the time to raise him.

Coming down the steps of an airplane, just arrived from Lisbon, a Granny disembarks. She is shakily stroking the pleats of her black native costume. Her wrinkled face shows the stress from an adventure so different from her usual rhythm of life in Calheta, a quiet fishing village at the outskirts of Madeira, Portugal. Her frail shrunken body trembles with excitement and expectation. She looks around timidly, searching. Momentarily her faded water-blue eyes light up. A husky man lifts his Texan hat from a receding graying hairline and welcomes her with outstretched arms. Her son! Her little Juca! Tears of joy enhance her weathered face while the man places a soft tender kiss on her wrinkled forehead.

At the departure gate, a young couple lingers in tight embrace. The girlish figure of the woman shakes with hysteria. They've only been married for one month and now he has to go into the service. A kiss and yet another kiss is exchanged while they cling to each other. Then the young man tears himself away, straightens his youthful shoulders and walks stiffly to the gate. She remains glued to the large window, her nervous breath painting ringlets on the glass while she watches the plane disappear on the horizon. Tears begin to wet her face.

At the gift counter, a flaming redhead is sampling gold bracelets and sure enough an apparent sugar daddy, pulls out his wallet. It says "Bermuda" on their baggage tag. The young lady knows the odds. She is going to get as much out of the trip and out of him as possible.

Scene after scene plays on the airport stage. The noise of the planes becomes mere background music to the performance of human emotions. ✈

Romance Hasn't Died

It was on one of those long Africa trips out of New York — the ones you dreaded for the long in-flight hours and loved for the sun.

Our first layover was Robertsfield, Monrovia. It was a boring place, with little else to do but to have a debriefing party. My husband Ray and Bob, the engineer, were the only male crew members with us on the layover. The Captain and First Officer had continued with the plane to Accra, Ghana. We decided to tease Bob with "When is the engagement party?" because we had noticed that he had an eye on Lynn, one of our stewardesses.

I wonder if Lynn and Bob would ever have looked at each other if not for the sweltering African air. The first two days passed with Lynn and Bob teasing each other, finding faults in each other till it developed into a mutual hate/love relationship.

Luck was with them. Our airplane broke down in Accra saving us from going to Dar es Salem, Tanzania, while providing a great opportunity to again plan a debriefing party after a somewhat tense landing in Accra. Our operating crew had come in with the plane that had picked us up in Robertsfield. They too had gotten off in Accra. So why not make it an engagement party? Our stewardess, Carol, and the first officer, Harold, bought gin for $1.75 in Accra City. It smelled like turpentine and tasted like rotten potatoes. That did not diminish the fun. Surprisingly, nobody got sick from it either. Bob had made a beautiful engagement ring from a plastic band covering the rim of a salt shaker and a 7-carat light bulb from a flashlight to top it off. It was touching to see how delighted Lynn was with it and nobody could have gotten a more affectionate kiss for a real gem than Bob got for his invention.

Even at your engagement party, you cannot just hold hands all evening, especially if you have guests. Carol came up with the idea of a body-painting party. I had my arm decorated in colorful watercolor ornaments declaring peace and love, and our stewardess Susan who wore a dress cut out in the waistline was painted in a beautiful dark brown and purple to cover the nakedness. I bet the maid had never seen so many different colors on the dirty towels before when she collected them the next day to be laundered.

```
BEND AND PEEL

  PAN AM  MAINTENANCE REQUIRED

REASON_____
_____
_____

FLT. NO._____      SEGMENT_____
DATE_____      SIGN_____
P/N 872-177615A            Ptd. in U.S.A.        4-81
```

Maintenance advised us that the plane was to be ferried. We were expected to stay for three days in Accra and then turn around back to Monrovia. To give the lovers some time, they were excused from the party that evening but not before the date for their wedding had been set for Sunday, 48 hours before our new departure time. Sandy, who had majored in arts drew up a truly authentic looking marriage license, which we sealed with a stamp from Germany and authorized with a fake signature of Head Chief Lumumba and the true signature of our captain who, to say the least, was a good sport all along.

My husband Ray performed the ceremony. Dressed in a white shirt worn backward, my oversized blue sunglasses and carrying a Bible, he was the image of authority. Lynn was pale and serious when it was her turn to say "I do" and Bob had the runs even before the wedding ceremony began. As wedding gifts, the couple received an artistically painted cup, 20 Rials, and a flower bouquet improvised by a silk scarf printed with flowers. Of course, the groom presented a wedding band in perfect match to the engagement ring. From that evening on, the two lovebirds referred to each other only as man and wife. I don't know if Lynn and Bob continued their courtship after the trip. For sure we had had a ball and proved once again what innovative and fun-loving traits could be found among the people of the Pan Am family. ✈

Missed Opportunity

Life is tricky. Sometimes it throws us golden threads. If we don't grab those immediately, they will be gone forever.

A month of flying to Paris. The last trip for the month. I was going to have my hair done. Had no particular hairdresser in mind and so I called one close to our layover hotel.

This story takes place in 1963. As a bit of background, my mother and my father had been divorced during World War II and all connections had been ended. My father's first marriage produced a daughter who was killed in a bobsled accident. My father had to leave Berlin, my hometown, in 1942 to flee from Hitler. He ended up in Paris. I never believed that my father had not tried to make contact with me but that does not change the happening of the day I am now writing about.

Anyhow, I called the hairdresser from the hotel and asked for an appointment around 3 pm.

"We have you down for 11 am," I was told when I gave my name.

My maiden name is Hungarian and not so easy to confuse with any other. I explained that is impossible since we only landed a half an hour ago at Orly Airport. I had not yet called anybody. They had no other times available.

 My French, bad as it is, did not allow me any further discussion, so I decided to call another salon. Much later that day, I put two and two together. The other woman with the same quite possibly was my stepsister. I had missed meeting her at the salon by a hair. ✈

What a fun FaceBook group for sharing memories. Following are some of the posts I've shared over the years.

Independence Day

Published July 1 in South Bay Neighbor

I spent a lifetime probing and searching
For things about which the critiques sing
Like fantasies, facts truth or lie
So for today I chose the Fourth of July.

Around the world I many times flew
Skimming the firmament when gray turned to blue.
In many places I have been
The Seven Wonders I have seen.

I socialized with the poor and the rich
Visited the Taj Mahal and the London Bridge.
Year after year on Independence Day
I joined into the cheers and firework play.

Thus again I hope to elevate your feeling
Cause melodious chants to hit the ceiling.
I want to relay the written word just right
Pass on positive ideas that spread delight.

Finally now having reached advanced age
I found what all along I had wanted to stage.
With my mind open though my body remiss
I wish that you all experience this day's bliss.

Would you agree this is a little while ago?
It will never come again

A passenger on one of the first jets Pan Am had, did this drawing after we had him well fed with caviar and champagne. He did this with a few strokes and in a few minutes on a Pan Am menu. I forgot his name but I will never forget what wonderful times I had working the First Class.

Went to a Kabuki Performance during a layover in Tokyo, September 1970. Those were the times. Shows in every capital of the world.

At one time I had the world in my hands. On a public relations assignment for Pan Am. At the Berlin ticket office.
Following that I saw the world and now I am doing my best to fit into this world.

In-Flight Memories

I am browsing through old Pan Am documents and pictures. Going thru the menus, which were always in demand I just came across one with a personal note to me "with good wishes" by Ted Kennedy.

I remember vividly going to his seat, he was sitting right behind the bulkhead in Economy class and asking him to please sign the menu for me, which he graciously did. What surprised me then was that he was sitting back there and not in First Class. He was an Excor on our passenger list and his rank and position in politics certainly would have warranted a First Class seat.

I found out that this had been arranged on purpose. It was to show the masses that Politicians did not spend the folk's money but knew how to be prudent.

Oh well, I have thought about that many times lately, when Politicians nowadays fly in their own jets and take advantage of their positions in many ways. How times change.

We all were very proud and I know that this feeling has remained with many of us for good.

Back on earth after a long flight.
Die Erde hat mich wieder!

PAN AM DID IT ALL!!!

Five men and a woman

Five women and a man

Remember the Military Charters.! Heartache, joy, Pan Am made it possible for us to experience it all. Forever grateful in memory!

This is from a cover of Pan Am Magazine that we used to put into the seat pockets on the planes. The same pockets that used to hold those paper bags when there was no pressurization, like on the DC 4 or DC 6. Barf bags we used to call them

Having lived here since the day I started Pan Am I come across items from Pan Am greeting me daily! Memories are made from this.

All the items from Pan Am that are around my house keep my memory fresh. It seems like yesterday that the world was at my fingertips for picking where to go from the monthly schedules.

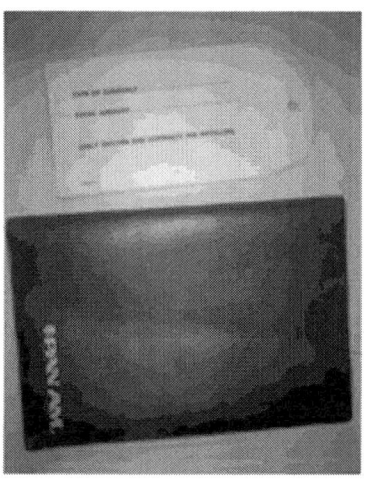

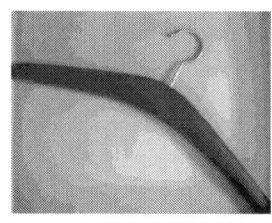

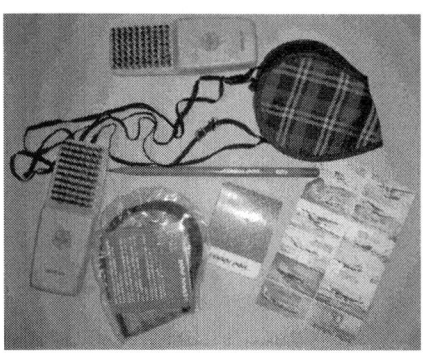

Remember the hangers we had in First class. Fur coats swept behind, leather coats in three different colors handed to me by a trio of girl singers, a writer's raccoon coat handed over with a smile.

One could have gotten jealous but no, not the Pan Am crew. Smiling is all we had on our minds –believe it or not.

Ivory Shop 1960 Liberia Monrovia- I spent weeks in the Firestone Hospital during a layover. They kept me drugged. Another not yet written experience from my not yet written book!

Those good old times were really good old times.

It was a year after I had been hired. I was flying out of New York. One year was all I wanted to fly. This picture was taken at a public relations assignment from Pan Am. 25 years later I was still flying. Sure some of you can relate to this. Let's hear your stories.

Body Image: When flying as cabin attendant for Pan Am I had to smile even when I did not feel like it.
A stewardess was to be seen by passengers as slim, trim and relaxed. No matter what you really felt, what troubled you was not to be detected. You were trained not to let your voice, your attitude or your demeanor give you away. There was only one body image: "The Smiling Stewardess"✈

Red Skelton

August 8, 1957

Dear Mr. Rodrigues:

My family and I want to thank you for your kindness in making our flight so enjoyable.

Your courtesy and friendship were most helpful and appreciated by all of us.

Warmest regards,

Red Skelton

Red Skelton and family

RS:md

Mr. Raymond Rodrigues
21-32 Prospect Avenue
Bronx, New York

Tears

I had thought a poem on this subject could spend tribute
But now – suddenly, I am not in the mood.
So in prose I will cover the task
Before in tears of frustration I bask.

The midnight sun is setting over the little fishing village in Cascais, Portugal. A day's work has come to an end. Some haggard weather-beaten fishermen are already preparing for their morning outing. The nets have to be stacked. A couple of reassuring words must be exchanged with the wives. For this poor village, fishing is a life necessity. Men must go out, and come back with a good catch. The sea does not always cooperate with the fishermen. Often lives are in danger. Sharks have infested the waters, which reminds me of my times with Pan American when one of our jets plunged into the Caribbean Sea at Caracas, Venezuela.

Rescuers had found inflated life rafts during the search, indicating some of the passengers had survived the explosion. They must have gotten out of the aircraft into the shark-infested waters. It is gruesome to imagine what most likely had occurred. Survival so close inside. A dreadful death met those people only a few minutes after escaping from the burning, sinking hull of the once proud airliner.

Is it fate? As a rule, I do not believe in the que sera, sera. It just happened to the crew on duty that day. It could have happened to anybody else. It could have happened to me! The male cabin attendant on that particular flight, Al Perez, was an old-timer who had flown the world for more than 20 years. He was a man who strictly adhered to company rules.

A friendly, warm-hearted man in his 40s, he had been involved in another crash long before the jet planes entered aviation. At that time, he had been among a few survivors. I am convinced that also this time he was among those who escaped from the airplane.

Sharks had been steered to the crash site attracted by the blood, making survival efforts for the passengers useless. Ironically, Al Perez was not supposed to be on that flight at all. He had picked this particular assignment from the open time board and gotten it due to his high seniority. Was this his fate? On this same plane, there was also a junior stewardess, only 22 years old. She was still in flight training; this was her introductory flight. She too died after evacuating from the plane into the waters. Her body was never found. What agony her parents suffer!

Tears wet my cheeks. The recollection has made me cry. ✈

Let me off the birds

Now in the finale of this book, my confession: I was afraid of flying and consequently hated flying. The following will allow you an insight into my emotions whenever up in the air.

I have been afraid of flying all my life and many times wished, "Let me off the birds." Here is how I felt on one not-so-rare occasion. I am trying to concentrate on an assignment for a writing class I have signed up with but my mind wanders. I cannot stick with an imaginary problem while something real and pressing nags on me.

A letter has been received by the airline I am working for, predicting that three of their planes will be blown up in the near future. I fly on those planes. I am involved!

Naturally all kinds of precautions are being taken. The bags of all passengers are being checked, opened and checked again. Passengers have to submit to body checks and interrogations. The planes are guarded with gun-carrying officers. No unauthorized person is allowed near. Yet all these efforts seem to be so futile.

There are a great number of ways threats like this could materialize into cruel reality. It is impossible to check all the cargo, all the packages, watch out for weird smells, recognize all unusual behavior by boarding passengers. What kind of person is it anyhow that would thrive on killing innocent people en masse? Terrorists, fanatics, suicide candidates? What do those persons have in common that makes them stand out in a crowd? Mostly nothing until it is too late.

It is hopefully just a hoax, a well-planned scheme to cause uproar in the scheduled functioning of the airline. Three planes within the routes of the United States were mentioned in the letter. Which planes? What dates? Where? It was said that the date was anticipated between December 24 and December 27. During this time approximately 3,000 take-offs and landings will be conducted by my airline alone. It would be unthinkable to ground an entire fleet because of a threat.

I am not a hero, and I do not believe in *que sera, sera*. I am scheduled to go on a flight this evening leaving New York's JFK International Airport westbound to Caracas, Venezuela. The fact that one of our planes has crashed only 10 days ago does not help.

Yet there is hope because if I were really convinced that something dreadful was going to happen, I could cancel out. Nobody can force me to take that flight tonight. I am getting ready to go. My suitcase is packed and my uniform is hanging on the bedroom door all pressed and adorned with my clipper wings. I feel like a hero now but if I come back on the 26th and reread these pages, then I will probably feel quite ridiculous. Yet there remains the question – Will I?"

Reading this now in 2013, I assume it was written about 1969. Forty-five years have passed. After that day I continued to fly until 1985. In 1990, my airline folded. Several airplane tragedies have occurred in the meantime: Lockerbie, Scotland, and the Twin Towers being the worst.

My last flight as stewardess was in 1985. One more flight after that, as passenger to be with my mother in her last hours. That was it. I have tried different kinds of therapy, classes and self-motivation. No success. I am still afraid of flying and nothing can get me into an airplane anymore.

2015: Several in-flight accidents have happened since I last edited this piece. A pilot died at the controls. A flight disappeared and could not be found. A pilot committed suicide and crashed his plane into the mountains. I would prefer of course that all this could have been avoided but it certainly does not help to make me change my personal feelings about flying.

2016: Circumstances change frighteningly fast. With the tense World situation due to ISIS, flying has become even more a matter of concern for many. More crashes, more diversions due to received warnings. Who can look forward to flying for pleasure!?

When the Malaysian accident happened In March 2014, I sat for hours in front of CNN on television. I had to think of my mother's comment many years back: "The pilots are not suicide candidates. They would notify if they suspected danger."

Well this issue was brought up during the investigation and search in the Indian Ocean.

I would gladly accept that my fear of flying had been silly and childish. Unfortunately, whenever one of these accidents happens, it proves me justified.

At 30,000 feet, the ocean beneath.
We are losing altitude.
I am afraid.
Well trained, I put on my frozen stewardess smile and begin to serve coffee to the passengers.
All the while aware of
"What will be, will be."

Sure the fact that flying is one of the safest means of transportation is correct. Maybe, had I been a pilot and not only Flight Attendant, the panicky moments caused by my being a control freak would have been mitigated.

My original fear of flying was the result of bombers waking me during the night. Squadrons of planes filling the night sky. It was World War II. Like veterans of wars return home with traumatic experiences that hamper their lifestyle for years, so my first encounter with air force bomber planes seems to have caused my fear of flying.

It is what it is. I take credit for 25 years in the air. I loved my job, but I did not love flying.

An incident with a tragic outcome took place a few days ago here on Long Island. A private plane crashed into a residential home. The homeowner was killed.

Often, I used such scenario as ending meaning it to be a joke by saying, "All I need is a plane to crash into my house and kill me." I would die in plane crash. No further comment.✈

Also Published

Infatuation: Poems of the Heart
An anthology of more than 60 love poems
By Alexandra H. Rodrigues (2015)
Available from Amazon and Kindle

Sprinkles: Personal Quotes
By Alexandra H. Rodrigues (2016)
Available from Amazon and Kindle

Her writings can also be found in

Abracadabra Children Bedtime Stories
American Poet Volume 1
Best Poets of 2014 Volume 2
Best Poets of 2015
Cocktailmolly
Eber & Wein
Famous Poets of the Heartland
Famous Poets Press
Great Poems of the Western World
Great South Bay Magazine
Love is like Air
Massapequa Public Library
My Social Book Volumes 1 and 2
Our 50 Most Famous Poets
Pan Am Historical Foundation
Pan Am Wing Tips Magazine
Postcard Stories
South Bay's Neighbor Poet's Corner
The Creativity Webzine
Trumpets to Heaven

AUG 2017

$14.99

Massapequa Public Library
523 Central Avenue
Massapequa, NY 11758
(516) 798-4607

65265388R00108

Made in the USA
Charleston, SC
18 December 2016